By what code do we live our sexual lives? In this work Russell sets out a new morality less distorting to human personality but nonetheless careful of social needs, in keeping with the emancipation of women and the development of contraceptives. Are we now living it? Or has conventional morality largely kept its hold?

Whatever one's ideas on the subject they can hardly fail to be clarified by reading Russell's book. Every aspect, from the origin of marriage to the value of a healthy sex life, from the influence of religion to the possibilities of eugenics, receives the incisive scrutiny of Bertrand Russell's intellect. Here is the Passionate Sceptic at his most vigorous.

Marriage and Morals

BY BERTRAND RUSSELL

1896 *German Social Democracy*
1897 *An Essay on the Foundations of Geometry* (Constable)
1900 *The Philosophy of Leibniz*
1903 *The Principles of Mathematics*
1910 *Philosophical Essays*
1912 *Problems of Philosophy* (Oxford U.P.)
1910-13 *Principia Mathematica* 3 vols. (with A. N. Whitehead) (Cambridge U.P.)
1914 *Our Knowledge of the External World*
1916 *Justice in Wartime* (out of print)
1916 *Principles of Social Reconstruction*
1917 *Political Ideals*
1918 *Roads to Freedom*
1918 *Mysticism and Logic*
1919 *Introduction to Mathematical Philosophy*
1920 *The Practice and Theory of Bolshevism*
1921 *The Analysis of Mind*
1922 *The Problem of China*
1923 *The Prospects of Industrial Civilization* (with Dora Russell)
1923 *The ABC of Atoms* (out of print)
1924 *Icarus or the Future of Science* (Spokesman Books)
1925 *The ABC of Relativity*
1926 *On Education*
1927 *An Outline of Philosophy*
1927 *The Analysis of Matter* (out of print)
1928 *Sceptical Essays*
1929 *Marriage and Morals*
1930 *The Conquest of Happiness*
1931 *The Scientific Outlook* (out of print)
1932 *Education and the Social Order*
1934 *Freedom and Organization: 1814-1914*
1935 *In Praise of Idleness*
1935 *Religion and Science* (Oxford U.P.)
1936 *Which Way to Peace?* (out of print)
1937 *The Amberley Papers* (with Patricia Russell)
1938 *Power*
1940 *An Inquiry into Meaning and Truth*
1945 *History of Western Philosophy*
1948 *Human Knowledge: Its Scope and Limits*
1949 *Authority and the Individual*

1950 *Unpopular Essays*
1951 *New Hopes for a Changing World* (out of print)
1952 *The Impact of Science on Society*
1953 *The Good Citizen's Alphabet* (Gaberbocchus)
1953 *Satan in the Suburbs* (out of print)
1954 *Nightmares of Eminent Persons* (out of print)
1954 *Human Society in Ethics and Politics*
1956 *Logic and Knowledge* (ed. by R. C. Marsh)
1956 *Portraits from Memory*
1957 *Why I Am Not a Christian* (ed. by Paul Edwards)
1957 *Understanding History and Other Essays* (USA only) (out of print)
1958 *Vital Letters of Russell, Khrushchev, Dulles* (out of print)
1958 *Bertrand Russell's Best* (ed. by Robert Egner)
1959 *Common Sense and Nuclear Warfare* (out of print)
1959 *Wisdom of the West* (ed. by Paul Foulkes) (Macdonald)
1959 *My Philosophical Development*
1959 *Bertrand Russell Speaks his Mind* (out of print)
1961 *Fact and Fiction*
1961 *Has Man a Future?*
1961 *The Basic Writings of Bertrand Russell* (ed. by R. E. Egner & L. Denonn)
1963 *Unarmed Victory*
1967 *War Crimes in Vietnam* (out of print)
1967 *The Archives of Bertrand Russell* (ed. by B. Feinberg, Continuum) (out of print)
1967 *Autobiography 1872-1914*
1968 *Autobiography 1914-1944*
1969 *Autobiography 1944-1967*
1969 *Dear Bertrand Russell . . .* (ed. by B. Feinberg & R. Kastrils)
1972 *The Collected Stories of Bertrand Russell* (ed. by B. Feinberg)
1973 *Essays in Analysis* (ed. by Douglas Lackey)
1973 *Bertrand Russell's America* (by Barry Feinberg and Ronald Kasrils)
1975 *Morals and Others* (ed. by Harry Ruja)
1983 *The Collected Papers of Bertrand Russell* Vol. 1
1984 *The Collected Papers of Bertrand Russell* Vol. 7

May, 1987

Marriage and Morals

BERTRAND RUSSELL

London
UNWIN PAPERBACKS
Boston   Sydney

First published in 1929
Twelfth impression 1958
First published in Unwin Books 1961
Seventh impression 1972
First published by Unwin Paperbacks 1976
Re-issued 1985

UNWIN ® PAPERBACKS
40 Museum Street, London WC1A 1LU, UK

Unwin Paperbacks
Park Lane, Hemel Hempstead, Herts HP2 4TE, UK

George Allen & Unwin Australia Pty Ltd
8 Napier Street, North Sydney, NSW 2060, Australia

Unwin Paperbacks with the
Port Nicholson Press
PO Box 11-838 Wellington, New Zealand

ISBN 0 04 173005 4

Set in 11 point Plantin
Made and printed in Great Britain by the
Guernsey Press Co. Ltd., Guernsey, Channel Islands.

Contents

Chapter 1

Introduction

In characterising a society, whether ancient or modern, there are two elements, rather closely interconnected, which are of prime importance: one is the economic system, the other the family system. There are at the present day two influential schools of thought, one of which derives everything from an economic source, while the other derives everything from a family or sexual source, the former school that of Marx, the latter that of Freud. I do not myself adhere to either school, since the interconnection of economics and sex does not appear to me to show any clear primacy of the one over the other from the point of view of causal efficacy. For example: no doubt the industrial revolution has had and will have a profound influence upon sexual morals, but conversely the sexual virtue of the Puritans was psychologically necessary as a part cause of the industrial revolution. I am not prepared myself to assign primacy to either the economic or the sexual factor, nor in fact can they be separated with any clearness. Economics is concerned essentially with obtaining food, but food is seldom wanted among human beings solely for the benefit of the individual who obtains it; it is wanted for the sake of the family, and as the family system changes, economic motives also change. It must be obvious that not only life insurance but most forms of private saving would nearly cease if children were taken away from their parents and brought up by the State as in Plato's Republic; that is to say, if the State were to adopt the role of the father, the State would, *ipso facto*, become the sole capitalist. Thoroughgoing Communists have often maintained the converse, that if the State is to be the sole capitalist, the family, as we have known it, cannot survive; and even if this is thought to go too far, it is impossible to deny an intimate connection between private property and the family, a connection which is reciprocal, so that we cannot say that one is cause and the other is effect.

The sexual morals of the community will be found to consist of several layers. There are first the positive institutions embodied in law; such, for example, as monogamy in some countries and polygamy in others. Next there is a layer where law does not intervene but public opinion is emphatic. And lastly there is a layer which is left to individual discretion, in practice if not in theory. There is no country in the world and there has been no age in the world's history where sexual ethics and sexual institutions have been determined by rational considerations, with the exception of Soviet Russia. I do not mean to imply that the institutions of Soviet Russia are in this respect perfect; I mean only that they are not the outcome of superstition and tradition, as are, at least in part, the institutions of all other countries in all ages. The problem of determining what sexual morality would be best from the point of view of general happiness and well-being is an extremely complicated one, and the answer will vary according to a number of circumstances. It will be different in an industrially advanced community from what it would be in a primitive agricultural régime. It will be different where medical science and hygiene are effective in producing a low death-rate from what it would be where plagues and pestilences carry away a large proportion of the population before it becomes adult. Perhaps when we know more, we shall be able to say that the best sexual ethic will be different in one climate from what it would be in another, and different again with one kind of diet from what it would be with another.

The effects of a sexual ethic are of the most diverse kinds -- personal, conjugal, familial, national and international. It may well happen that the effects are good in some of these respects, where they are bad in others. All must be considered before we can decide what on the balance we are to think of a given system. To begin with the purely personal: these are the effects considered by psychoanalysis. We have here to take account not only of the adult behaviour inculcated by a code, but also of the early education designed to produce obedience to the code, and in this region, as everyone knows, the effects of early taboos may be very curious and indirect. In this department of the subject we are at the level of personal well-being. The next stage of our problem arises when we consider the relations of men and women. It is clear that some sex relations have more value than others. Most people would agree that a sex relation is better when it has a large psychical element than when it is purely physical. Indeed, the view which has passed from the poets into the common consciousness of civilised men and women is that love increases in value in proportion as more of the personalities of the people concerned enters into the relation. The poets also have taught many people to value love in proportion to its intensity; this, however, is a more debatable matter. Most moderns would agree that love should be an equal relation, and that on this ground, if on no other, polygamy, for example, cannot be regarded as an ideal system. Throughout this department of the subject it is necessary to consider both marriage and extra-marital relations, since whatever system of marriage prevails, extra-marital relations will vary correspondingly.

We come next to the question of the family. There have existed in various times and places many different kinds of family groups, but the patriarchal family has a very large preponderance, and, moreover, the monogamic patriarchal family has prevailed more and more over the polygamic. The primary motive of sexual ethics as they have existed in Western civilisation since pre-Christian times has been to secure that degree of female virtue without which the patriarchal family becomes impossible, since paternity is

uncertain. What has been added to this in the way of insistence
on male virtue by Christianity had its psychological source
in asceticism, although in quite recent times this motive has
been reinforced by female jealousy, which became potent
with the emancipation of women. This latter motive seems,
however, to be temporary, since, if we may judge by ap-
pearances, women will tend to prefer a system allowing freedom to both sexes rather than one imposing upon men the
restrictions which hitherto have been suffered only by
women.

Within the monogamic family there are, however, many
varieties. Marriages may be decided by the parties themselves
or by their parents. In some countries the bride is purchased;
in others, e.g. France, the bridegroom. Then there may be all
kinds of differences as regards divorce, from the Catholic extreme, which permits no divorce, to the law of old China,
which permitted a man to divorce his wife for being a chat-
terbox. Constancy or quasi-constancy in sex relations arises
among animals, as well as among human beings, where, for
the preservation of the species, the participation of the male is
necessary for the rearing of the young. Birds, for example,
have to sit upon their eggs continuously to keep them warm,
and also have to spend a good many hours of the day getting
food. To do both is, among many species, impossible for one
bird, and therefore male co-operation is essential. The consequence is that most birds are models of virtue. Among human
beings the co-operation of the father is a great biological advantage to the offspring, especially in unsettled times and
among turbulent populations, but with the growth of modern
civilisation the role of the father is being increasingly taken
over by the State, and there is reason to think that a father
may cease before long to be biologically advantageous, at any
rate in the wage-earning class. If this should occur, we must
expect a complete breakdown of traditional morality, since
there will no longer be any reason why a mother should wish

the paternity of her child to be indubitable. Plato would have us go a step further, and put the State not only in place of the father but in that of the mother also. I am not myself sufficiently an admirer of the State, or sufficiently impressed with the delights of orphan asylums, to be enthusiastically in favour of this scheme. At the same time it is not impossible that economic forces may cause it to be to some extent adopted.

The law is concerned with sex in two different ways: on the one hand to enforce whatever sexual ethic is adopted by the community in question, and on the other hand to protect the ordinary rights of individuals in the sphere of sex. The latter have two main departments: on the one hand the protection of females and non-adults from assault and from harmful exploitation, on the other hand the prevention of venereal disease. Neither of these is commonly treated purely on its merits, and for this reason neither is so effectively dealt with as it might be. In regard to the former, hysterical campaigns about the White Slave Traffic lead to the passage of laws easily evaded by professional malefactors, while affording opportunities of blackmail against harmless people. In regard to the latter, the view that venereal disease is a just punishment for sin prevents the adoption of the measures which would be the most effective on purely medical grounds, while the general attitude that venereal disease is shameful causes it to be concealed, and therefore not promptly or adequately treated.

We come next to the question of population. This is in itself a vast problem which must be considered from many points of view. There is the question of the health of mothers, the question of the health of children, the question of the psychological effects of large and small families respectively upon the character of children. These are what may be called the hygienic aspects of the problem. Then there are the economic aspects, both personal and public: the question of the wealth

per head of a family or a community in relation to the size of
the family or the birth-rate of the community. Closely connected with this is the bearing of the population question
upon international politics and the possibility of world peace.
And finally there is the eugenic question as to the improvement or deterioration of the stock through the different birth
and death rates of the different sections of the community. No
sexual ethic can be either justified or condemned on solid
grounds until it has been examined from all the points of view
above enumerated. Reformers and reactionaries alike are in
the habit of considering one or at most two of the aspects of
the problem. It is especially rare to find any combination
of the private and the political points of view, and yet it is
quite impossible to say that either of these is more important
than the other, and we can have no assurance *a priori* that a
system which is good from a private point of view would also
be good from a political point of view, or vice versa. My own
belief is that in most ages and in most places obscure psychological forces have led men to adopt systems involving quite
unnecessary cruelty, and that this is still the case among the
most civilised races at the present day. I believe also that the
advances in medicine and hygiene have made changes in
sexual ethics desirable both from a private and public point of
view, while, as already suggested, the increasing role of the
State in education is gradually rendering the father less important than he has been throughout historical times. We
have, therefore, a twofold task in criticising the current
ethics: on the one hand we have to eliminate the elements of
superstition, which are often subconscious; on the other
hand we have to take account of those entirely new factors
which make the wisdom of past ages the folly instead of the
wisdom of the present.

In order to obtain a perspective upon the existing system, I
shall first consider some systems which have existed in the past
or exist at the present time among the less civilised portions of

mankind. I shall then proceed to characterise the system now in vogue in Western civilisation, and finally to consider the respects in which this system should be amended and the grounds for hoping that such amendment will take place.

Chapter 2

Matrilineal Societies

Marriage customs have always been a blend of three factors, which may be loosely called instinctive, economic, and religious respectively. I do not mean that these can be sharply distinguished, any more than they can in other spheres. The fact that shops are closed on Sundays has a religious origin, but is now an economic fact, and so it is with many laws and customs in relation to sex. A useful custom which has a religious origin will often survive on account of its utility after the religious basis has been undermined. The distinction between what is religious and what is instinctive is also a difficult one to make. Religions which have any very strong hold over men's actions have generally some instinctive basis. They are distinguished, however, by the importance of tradition, and by the fact that, among the various kinds of actions which are instinctively possible, they give a preference to certain kinds; for example, love and jealousy are both instinctive emotions, but religion has decreed that jealousy is a virtuous emotion to which the community ought to lend support, while love is at best excusable.

The instinctive element in sex relations is much less than is usually supposed. It is not my purpose in this book to go into anthropology except in so far as may be necessary to illustrate present-day problems, but there is one respect in which that science is very necessary for our purposes, and that is, to show how many practices, which we should have thought contrary to instinct, can continue for long periods without causing any great or obvious conflict with instinct. It has, for example, been a common practice not only with savages but with some comparatively civilised races, for virgins to be officially (and sometimes publicly) deflowered by priests. In Christian countries men have held that defloration should be the prerogative of the bridegroom, and most Christians, at any rate until recent times, would have regarded their repugnance to the custom of religious defloration as an instinctive one. The practice of lending one's wife to a guest as an act of hospitality is also one which to the modern European seems instinctively repugnant, and yet it has been very widespread. Polyandry is another custom which an unread white man would suppose contrary to human nature. Infanticide might seem still more so; yet the facts show that it is resorted to with great readiness wherever it seems economically advantageous. The fact is that, where human beings are concerned, instinct is extraordinarily vague and easily turned aside from its natural course. This is the case equally among savages and among civilised communities. The word 'instinct', in fact, is hardly the proper one to apply to anything so far from rigid as human behaviour in sexual matters. The only act in this whole realm which can be called instinctive in the strict psychological sense is the act of sucking in infancy. I do not know how it may be with savages, but civilised people have to learn to perform the sexual act. It is not uncommon for doctors to be asked by married couples of some years' standing for advice as to how to get children, and to find on examination that the couples have not known how to perform intercourse. The sexual act is not, therefore, in the strictest sense, instinctive, although of course there is a natural trend towards it and a desire not easily to be satisfied without it. Indeed, where human beings are concerned we do not have the precise behaviour-patterns which are to be found among other animals, an instinct in that sense is replaced by something rather different. What we have with human beings is first of all a dissatisfaction leading to activities of a more or less random and imperfect sort, but arriving gradually, more or less by accident, at an activity which gives satisfaction and which is therefore repeated. What is instinctive is thus not so much the finished activity as the impulse to learn it, and often the activity which would give satisfaction is by no means definitely pre-determined, though, as a rule, the biologically most advantageous activity will give the most complete satisfaction, provided it is learnt before contrary habits have been acquired.

Seeing that all civilised modern societies are based upon the patriarchal family, and that the whole conception of female virtue has been built up in order to make the patriarchal family possible, it is important to inquire what natural impulses have gone to produce the sentiment of paternity. This question is by no means so easy as unreflective persons might suppose. The feeling of a mother towards her child is one which it is not at all difficult to understand, since there is a close physical tie, at any rate up to the moment of weaning. But the relation of father to child is indirect, hypothetical and inferential: it is bound up with beliefs as to the virtue of the wife, and belongs accordingly to a region too intellectual to be regarded as properly instinctive. Or at least it would so seem if one supposed that the sentiment of paternity must be directed essentially towards a man's own children. This, however, is by no means necessarily the case. The Melanesians do not know that people have fathers, yet among them fathers are at least as fond of their children as they are where they know them to be their children. A flood of light has been thrown upon the psychology of paternity by Malinowski's books on the Trobriand Islanders. Three books especially – *Sex and Repression in Savage Society, The Father in Primitive Psychology*, and *The Sexual Life of Savages in North-West Melanesia* – are quite indispensable to any understanding of the complex sentiment which we call that of paternity. There are, in fact, two entirely distinct reasons which may lead a man to be interested in a child: he may be interested in the child because he believes it to be his child, or again he may be interested in it because he knows it to be his wife's child. The second of these motives alone operates where the part of the father in generation is not known.

The fact that among the Trobriand Islanders people are not known to have fathers has been established by Malinowski beyond question. He found, for example, that when a man has been away on a voyage for a year or more and finds on his return that his wife has a new-born child, he is delighted, and quite unable to understand the hints of Europeans suggesting doubts as to his wife's virtue. What is perhaps still more convincing, he found that a man who possessed a superior breed of pigs would castrate all the males, and be unable to understand that this involved a deterioration of the breed. It is thought that spirits bring children and insert them into their mothers. It is recognised that virgins cannot conceive, but this is supposed to be because the hymen presents a physical barrier to the activities of the spirits. Unmarried men and girls live a life of complete free love, but, for some unknown reason, unmarried girls very seldom conceive. Oddly enough, it is considered disgraceful when they do so, in spite of the fact that, according to native philosophy, nothing they have done is responsible for their becoming pregnant. Sooner or later a girl grows tired of variety and marries. She goes to live in her husband's village, but she and her children are still reckoned as belonging to the village from which she has come. Her husband is not regarded as having any blood relationship to the children, and descent is traced solely through the female line. The kind of authority over children which is elsewhere exercised by fathers is, among the Trobriand Islanders, vested in the maternal uncle. Here, however, a very curious complication comes in. The brother-and-sister taboo. is exceedingly severe, so that after they are grown up brother and sister can never talk together on any subject connected, however remotely, with sex. Consequently, although the maternal uncle has authority over the children, he sees little of them except when they are away from their mother and from home. This admirable system secures for the children a measure of affection without discipline which is unknown elsewhere. Their father plays with them and is nice to them but has not the right to order them about, whereas their maternal uncle, who has the right to order them about, has not the right to be on the spot.

Strangely enough, in spite of the belief that there is no blood tie between the child and its mother's husband, it is supposed that children resemble their mothers' husbands rather than their mothers or their brothers and sisters. Indeed, it is very bad manners to suggest a resemblance between a brother and sister, or between a child and its mother, and even the most obvious resemblances are fiercely denied. Malinowski is of opinion that the affection of fathers for their children is stimulated by this belief in a resemblance to the father rather than to the mother. He found the relation of father and son a more harmonious and affectionate one than it often is among civilised people, and, as might have been expected, he found no trace of the Oedipus complex.

Malinowski found it quite impossible, in spite of his best argumentative efforts, to persuade his friends on the islands that there is such a thing as paternity. They regarded this as a silly story invented by the missionaries. Christianity is a patriarchal religion, and cannot be made emotionally or intellectually intelligible to people who do not recognise fatherhood. Instead of 'God the Father' it would be necessary to speak of 'God the Maternal Uncle', but this does not give quite the right shade of meaning, since fatherhood implies both power and love, whereas in Melanesia the maternal uncle has the power and the father has the love. The idea that men are God's children is one which cannot be conveyed to the Trobriand Islanders since they do not think that anybody is the child of any male. Consequently, missionaries are compelled to tackle first the facts of physiology before they can go on to preach their religion. One gathers from Malinowski that they have no success in this initial task, and have, therefore, been quite unable to proceed to the teaching of the Gospel.

Malinowski maintains, and in this I think he must be right, that if a man remains with his wife during pregnancy and child-birth he has an instinctive tendency to be fond of the child when it is born, and this is the basis of the paternal sentiment. 'Human paternity', he says, 'which appears at first as almost completely lacking in biological foundation, can be shown to be deeply rooted in natural endowment and organic need.' He thinks, however, that if a man is absent from his wife during pregnancy he will not *instinctively* feel affection for the child at first, although, if custom and tribal ethics lead him to as-sociate with the mother and child, affection will develop as it would have done if he had been with the mother throughout. In all the important human relations, socially desirable acts, towards which there is an instinct not strong enough to be always compelling, are enforced by social ethics, and so it is among these savages. Custom enjoins that the mother's hus-band shall care for the children and protect them while they are young, and this custom is not difficult to enforce, since it is, as a rule, in line with instinct.

The instinct to which Malinowski appeals to explain the attitude of a father towards his children among the Mel-anesians is, I think, somewhat more general than it appears in his pages. There is, I think, in either a man or a woman a tendency to feel affection for any child whom he or she has to tend. Even if nothing but custom and convention, or wages, have in the first instance caused an adult to have the care of a child, the mere fact of having that care will, in the majority of cases, cause affection to grow up. No doubt this feeling is reinforced where the child is the child of a woman who is loved. It is, therefore, intelligible that these savages show considerable devotion to their wives' children, and it may be taken as certain that this is a large element in the affection which civilised men give to their children. Malinowski maintains – and it is difficult to see how his opinion can be controverted – that all mankind must have passed through the stage in which the Trobriand Islanders are now, since there must have been a period when paternity was nowhere recognised. Animal families, where they include a father, must have a like basis, since they cannot have any other. It is only among human beings, after the fact of fatherhood has become known, that the sentiment of paternity can assume the form with which we are familiar.

Chapter 3

Patriarchal Systems

As soon as the physiological fact of paternity is recognised, a quite new element enters into paternal feeling, an element which has led almost everywhere to the creation of patriarchal societies. As soon as a father recognises that the child is, as the Bible says, his 'seed', his sentiment towards the child is reinforced by two factors, the love of power and the desire to survive death. The achievements of a man's descendants are in a sense his achievements, and their life is a continuation of his life. Ambition no longer finds its termination at the grave, but can be indefinitely extended through the careers of descendants. Consider, for example, the satisfaction of Abraham when he is informed that his seed shall possess the land of Canaan. In a matrilineal society, family ambition would have to be confined to women, and as women do not do the fighting, such family ambition as they may have has less effect than that of men. One must suppose, therefore, that the discovery of fatherhood would make human society more competitive, more energetic, more dynamic and hustling than it had been in the matrilineal stage. Apart from this effect, which is to some extent hypothetical, there was a new and all-important reason for insisting upon the virtue of wives. The purely instinctive element in jealousy is not nearly so strong as most moderns imagine. The extreme strength of jealousy in patriarchal societies is due to the fear of falsification of descent. This may be seen in the fact that a man who is tired of his wife and passionately devoted to his mistress will nevertheless be more jealous where his wife is concerned than when he finds a rival to the affections of his mistress. A legitimate child is a continuation of a man's ego, and his affection for the child is a form of egoism. If, on the other hand, the child is not legitimate, the putative father is tricked into lavishing care upon a child with whom he has no biological connection. Hence the discovery of fatherhood led to the subjection of woman as the only means of securing their virtue – a subjection first physical and then mental, which reached its height in the Victorian age. Owing to the subjection of women, there has in most civilised communities been no genuine companionship between husbands and wives; their relation has been one of condescension on the one side and duty on the other. All the man's serious thoughts and purposes he has kept to himself, since robust thought might lead his wife to betray him. In most civilised communities women have been denied almost all experience of the world and of affairs. They have been kept artificially stupid and therefore uninteresting. From Plato's dialogues one derives an impression that he and his friends regarded men as the only proper objects of serious love. This is not to be wondered at when one considers that all the matters in which they were interested were completely closed to respectable Athenian women. Exactly the same state of affairs prevailed in China until recently, and in Persia in the great days of Persian poetry, and in many other ages and places. Love as a relation between men and women was ruined by the desire to make sure of the legitimacy of children. And not only love, but the whole contribution that women can make to civilisation, has been stunted for the same reason.

The economic system naturally changed at the same time that the method of reckoning descent was transformed. In a matrilineal society a man inherits from his maternal uncle; in a patrilineal society he inherits from his father. The relation of father and son in a patrilineal society is a closer one than

any relation between males which exists in a matrilineal
society, for, as we have seen, the functions which we naturally
attribute to the fathers are divided in a matrilineal society
between the father and the maternal uncle, affection and care
coming from the father, while power and property come from
the maternal uncle. It is clear, therefore, that the patriarchal
family is a more closely knit affair than the family of a more
primitive type.

It would seem that it is only with the introduction of the
patriarchal system that men came to desire virginity in their
brides. Where the matrilineal system exists young women sow
their wild oats as freely as young men, but this could not be
tolerated when it became of great importance to persuade
women that all intercourse outside marriage is wicked.

Fathers, having discovered the fact of their existence, proceeded everywhere to exploit it to the uttermost. The history
of civilisation is mainly a record of the gradual decay of paternal power, which reached its maximum, in most civilised
countries, just before the beginning of historical records. Ancestor worship, which has lasted to our own day in China and
Japan, appears to have been a universal characteristic of early
civilisation. A father had absolute power over his children,
extending in many cases, as in Rome, to life and death.
Daughters throughout civilisation, and sons in a great many
countries, could not marry without their fathers' consent, and
it was usual for the father to decide whom they should marry.
A woman had in no period of her life any independent existence, being subject first to her father and then to her husband. At the same time an old woman could exercise almost
despotic power within the household; her sons and their wives
all lived under the same roof with her, and her daughters-in-
law were completely subject to her. Down to the present day
in China it is not unknown for young married women to be
driven to suicide by the persecution of their mothers-in-law,
and what can still be seen in China is only what was universal

throughout the civilised parts of Europe and Asia until very recent times. When Christ said he was come to set the son against the father and the daughter-in-law against the mother-in-law, He was thinking of just such households as one still finds in the Far East. The power which the father acquired in the first instance by his superior strength was reinforced by religion, which may in most of its forms be defined as the belief that the gods are on the side of the Government. Ancestor worship, or something analogous, prevailed very widely. The religious ideas of Christianity, as we have already seen, are impregnated with the majesty of fatherhood. The monarchic and aristocratic organisation of society and the system of inheritance were based everywhere upon paternal power. In early days economic motives upheld this system. One sees in Genesis how men desired a numerous progeny, and how advantageous it was to them when they had it. Multiplication of sons was as advantageous as multiplication of flocks and herds. That was why in those days Yahveh ordered men to increase and multiply.

But as civilisation advanced the economic circumstances changed, so that the religious precepts which had at one time been exhortations to self-interest began to grow irksome. After Rome became prosperous, the rich no longer had large families. Throughout the later centuries of Roman greatness the old patrician stocks were continually dying out in spite of the exhortations of moralists, which were as ineffective then as they are now. Divorce became easy and common; women in the upper classes achieved a position almost equal to that of men, and the *patria potestas* grew less and less. This development was in many ways very much like that of our own day, but it was confined to the upper classes, and shocked those who were not rich enough to profit by it. The civilisation of antiquity, in contrast to our own, suffered through being confined to a very small percentage of the population. It was this that made it precarious while it lasted, and caused it ultimately to succumb to a great uprush of superstition from below. Christianity and the barbarian invasion destroyed the Greco-Roman system of ideas. While the patriarchal system remained, and was even at first strengthened, as compared at any rate to the system of aristocratic Rome, it had nevertheless to accommodate itself to a new element, namely the Christian view of sex and the individualism derived from the Christian doctrine of the soul and salvation. No Christian community can be so frankly biological as the civilisations of antiquity and of the Far East. Moreover, the individualism of Christian communities gradually affected the policy of Christian countries, while the promise of personal immortality diminished the interest which men took in the survival of their progeny, which had formerly seemed to them the nearest approach to immortality that was possible. Modern society, although it is still patrilineal and although the family still survives, attaches infinitely less importance to paternity than ancient societies did. And the strength of the family is enormously less than it used to be. Men's hopes and ambitions nowadays are utterly different from those of the patriarchs in Genesis. They wish to achieve greatness rather through their position in the State than through the possession of a numerous posterity. This change is one of the reasons why traditional morals and theology have less force than they used to have. Nevertheless, the change itself is in fact a part of Christian theology. To see how this has come about, the way in which religion has affected men's views of marriage and the family must next be examined.

Chapter 4

Phallic Worship, Asceticism and Sin

From the time that the fact of paternity was first discovered, sex has always been a matter of great interest to religion. This is only what one would expect, since religion concerns itself with everything that is mysterious and important. Fruit-fulness, whether of crops, or of flocks and herds, or of women, was of prime importance to men in the beginnings of the agricultural and pastoral stages. Crops did not always flourish and intercourse did not always produce pregnancy. Religion and magic were invoked to make sure of the desired result. In accordance with the usual ideas of sympathetic magic, it was thought that by promoting human fertility the fertility of the soil could be encouraged; and human fertility itself, which was desired in many primitive communities, was promoted by various religious and magical ceremonies. In ancient Egypt, where agriculture appears to have risen before the end of the matrilineal epoch, the sexual element in religion was at first not phallic but concerned with the female genitalia, the shape of which was supposed to be suggested by the cowry shell, which accordingly was held to have magic powers and came to be used as currency. This stage, however, passed away, and in later Egypt, as in most ancient civilisations, the sexual element in religion took the form of phallic worship. A very good short account of the most salient facts in this connection will be found in a chapter by Robert Briffault in *Sex in Civilisation*.[1]

'Agricultural festivals [he says], and more especially those connected with the planting of seed and the gathering of harvest, present in every region of the world and in every age the most conspicuous examples of general sexual licence. . . . The agricultural populations of Algeria resent any restriction being placed upon the licentiousness of their women upon the ground that any attempt to enforce sexual morality would be prejudicial to the success of their agricultural operations. The Athenian *thesmophoria*, or sowing-feasts, preserved in an attenuated form the original character of the magic of fertility. The women carried phallic emblems and uttered obscenities. The *saturnalia* were the Roman feasts of sowing, and have been succeeded by the *carnival* of Southern Europe, in which phallic symbols, differing little from those in vogue among the Sioux and in Dahomey, were down to recent years a conspicuous feature.'[2]

In many parts of the world it has been thought that the moon (regarded as masculine) is the true father of all children.[3] This view is, of course, connected with moon worship. There has been a curious conflict, not directly relevant to our present subject, between lunar and solar priesthoods and lunar and solar calendars. The calendar has at all times played an important part in religion. In England down to the

---

[1] Edited by V. F. Claverton and S. D. Schmalhausen, with an introduction by Havelock Ellis. London: George Allen and Unwin Ltd, 1929.
[2] Briffault, *loc. cit.*, p. 34.
[3] In the Maori State 'the moon is the permanent husband or true husband of all women. According to the knowledge of our ancestors and elders, the marriage of man and wife is a matter of no moment: the moon is the true husband.' Similar views have existed in most parts of the world, and obviously represent a transition from the stage where paternity was unknown to the complete recognition of its importance. Briffault, *loc. cit.*, p. 37.

eighteenth century and in Russia down to the Revolution of
1917, an innaccurate calendar was perpetuated owing to the
feeling that the Gregorian calendar was papistical. Similarly,
the very inaccurate lunar calendars were everywhere advocated by priests devoted to the worship of the moon, and the
victory of the solar calendar was slow and partial. In Egypt this
conflict was at one time a source of civil war. One may suppose that it was connected with a grammatical dispute as to
the gender of the word 'moon', which has remained masculine
in German down to the present day. Both sun worship and
moon worship have left their traces in Christianity, since
Christ's birth occurred at the winter solstice, while His resur-
rection occurred at the Paschal full-moon. Although it is rash
to attribute any degree of rationality to primitive civilisation,
it is nevertheless difficult to resist the conclusion that the
victory of the sun worshippers, wherever it occurred, was due
to the patent fact that the sun has more influence than the
moon over the crops. Accordingly Saturnalia generally occurred in the spring.

Considerable elements of phallic worship existed in all the
pagan religions of antiquity, and supplied the Fathers with
many polemical weapons. In spite of their polemics, however,
traces of phallic worship survived throughout the Middle
Ages, and only Protestantism was finally successful in ex-
tirpating all vestiges of it.

'In Flanders and in France ithyphallic saints were not uncommon, such as St Giles in Brittany, St René in Anjou, St
Greluchon at Bourges, St Regnaud, St Arnaud. The most
popular throughout southern France, St Foutin, was reputed
to have been the first bishop of Lyons. When his shrine at
Embrun was destroyed by the Huguenots, the phenomenal
phallus of the holy personage was rescued from the ruins,
stained red from abundant libations of wine, which his worshippers had been in the habit of pouring over it, drinking

thereafter the potation as an infallible remedy against sterility and impotence.'[1]

Sacred prostitution is another institution which was very widespread in antiquity. In some places ordinary respectable women went to a temple and had intercourse either with a priest or with a casual stranger. In other cases, the priestesses themselves were sacred harlots. Probably all such customs arose out of the attempt to secure the fertility of women through the favour of the gods, or the fertility of the crops by sympathetic magic.

So far we have been considering pro-sexual elements in religion; anti-sexual elements, however, existed side by side with the others from a very early time, and in the end, wherever Christianity or Buddhism prevailed, these elements won a complete victory over their opposites. Westermarck[2] gives many instances of what he calls 'the curious notion that there is something impure and sinful in marriage, as in sexual relations generally.' In the most diverse parts of the world, quite remote from any Christian or Buddhist influence, there have been orders of priests and priestesses vowed to celibacy. Among the Jews the sect of the Essenes considered all sexual intercourse impure. This view seems to have gained ground in antiquity even in the circles most hostile to Christianity. There was indeed a general tendency towards asceticism in the Roman Empire. Epicureanism nearly died out and stoicism replaced it among cultivated Greeks and Romans. Many passages in the Apocrypha suggest an almost monkish attitude towards women, very different from the robust virility of the older books of the Old Testament. The neo-Platonists were almost as ascetic as the Christians. From Persia the doctrine that matter is evil spread to the West, and brought with it the belief that all sexual intercourse is impure. This is,

[1] Briffault *loc. cit.* p. 40.
[2] *History of Human Marriage*, pp. 151 ff.

though not in an extreme form, the view of the Church, but I do not wish to consider the Church until the next chapter. What is evident is that in certain circumstances men are led spontaneously to a horror of sex, and this when it arises is quite as much a natural impulse as the more usual attraction towards sex. It is necessary to take account of it and to understand it psychologically if we are to be able to judge what kind of sexual system is most likely to satisfy human nature.

It should be said to begin with that it is useless to look to beliefs as the source of this kind of attitude. Beliefs of this sort must be in the first place inspired by a mood; it is true that when once they exist they may perpetuate the mood, or at any rate actions in accordance with the mood, but it is hardly likely that they will be the prime causes of an anti-sexual attitude. The two main causes of such an attitude are, I should say, jealousy and sexual fatigue. Wherever jealousy is aroused, even if it be only faintly, the sexual act appears to us disgusting, and the appetite which leads to it loathsome. The purely instinctive man, if he could have his way, would have all women love him and him only; any love which they may give to other men inspires in him emotions which may easily pass into moral condemnation. Especially is this the case when the woman is his wife. One finds in Shakespeare, for example, that his men do not desire their wives to be passionate. The ideal woman, according to Shakespeare, is one who submits to her husband's embraces from a sense of duty, but would not think of having a lover, since sex in itself is disagreeable to her and is only endured because the moral law commands that it should be. The instinctive husband, when he finds that his wife has betrayed him, is filled with disgust against both her and her lover, and is apt to conclude that all sex is beastly. Especially will this be the case if he has become impotent through excess or old age. Since old men have in most societies more weight than the young, it is natural that the official and correct opinion on sexual matters should be not that of hot-headed youth.

Sexual fatigue is a phenomenon introduced by civilisation; it must be quite unknown among animals and very rare among uncivilised men. In a monogamic marriage it is unlikely to occur except in a very small degree, since the stimulus of novelty is required with most men to lead them to physiological excess. It is also unlikely to occur when women are free to refuse their favours, for, in that case, like female animals, they will demand courtship before each act of intercourse, and will not yield their favours until they feel that a man's passions are sufficiently stimulated. This purely instinctive feeling and behaviour has been rendered rare by civilisation. What has done most to eliminate it is the economic factor. Married women and prostitutes alike make their living by means of their sexual charms, and do not, therefore, only yield when their own instinct prompts them to do so. This had greatly diminished the part played by courtship, which is nature's safeguard against sexual fatigue. Consequently men who are not restrained by a fairly rigid ethic are apt to indulge to excess; this produces in the end a feeling of weariness and disgust, which leads naturally to ascetic convictions.

Where jealousy and sexual fatigue co-operate, as they often do, the strength of the anti-sexual passion may become very great. I think this is the main reason why asceticism is apt to grow up in very licentious societies.

Celibacy as an historical phenomenon has, however, other sources as well. Priests and priestesses dedicated to the service of divinities may be regarded as married to these divinities, and as therefore obliged to abstain from all intercourse with mortals. They will naturally be considered exceptionally holy, and thus an association is brought about between holiness and celibacy. Up to our own day in the Catholic Church, nuns are regarded as the brides of Christ. And this is certainly one of the reasons why it is thought wicked for them to have intercourse with mortals.

I suspect that other causes more obscure than any we have yet considered had to do with the increasing ascetism of the ancient world in its later days. There are epochs when life seems cheerful, when men are vigorous, and when the joys of this mundane existence are sufficient to give complete satisfaction. There are other epochs when men seem weary, when this world and its joys do not suffice, and when men look to spiritual consolation or a future life to make up for the natural emptiness of this sublunary scene. Compare the Solomon of the 'Song of Songs' with the Solomon of Ecclesiastes; the one represents the ancient world in its prime, the other in its decay. What is the cause of this difference I do not profess to know. Perhaps it is something very simple and physiological, such as the substitution of a sedentary urban life for an active life in the open air; perhaps the Stoics had sluggish livers; perhaps the author of Ecclesiastes thought that all is vanity because he did not take enough exercise. However that may be, there is no doubt that a mood such as this leads easily to a condemnation of sex. Probably the causes we have suggested, and various others also, contributed to the general weariness of the later centuries of antiquity, and of this weariness asceticism was one feature. Unfortunately it was in this decadent and morbid period that the Christian ethic was formulated. The vigorous men of later periods have had to do their best to live up to an outlook on life belonging to diseased, weary and disillusioned men who had lost all sense of biological values and of the continuity of human life. This topic, however, belongs to our next chapter.

Chapter 5

Christian Ethics

'Marriage', says Westermarck, 'is rooted in family rather than family in marriage.' This view would have been a truism in pre-Christian times, but since the advent of Christianity it has become an important proposition needing to be stated with emphasis. Christianity, and more particularly St Paul, introduced an entirely novel view of marriage, that it existed not primarily for the procreation of children, but to prevent the sin of fornication.

The views of St Paul on marriage are set forth, with a clarity that leaves nothing to be desired, in the First Epistle to the Corinthians. The Corinthian Christians, one gathers, had adopted the curious practice of having illicit relations with their stepmothers (1 Cor. v. 1), and he felt the situation needed to be dealt with emphatically. The views which he set forth are as follows[1]:

'1. Now concerning the things whereof ye wrote unto me: It is good for a man not to touch a woman.

2. Nevertheless, to avoid fornication, let every man have his own wife, and let every woman have her own husband.

3. Let the husband render unto the wife due benevolence: and likewise also the wife unto the husband.

4. The wife hath not power of her own body, but the husband: and likewise also the husband hath not power of his own body, but the wife.

[1] I Cor. vii. 1–9

5. Defraud ye not one the other, except it be with consent for a time, that ye may give yourselves to fasting and prayer; and come together again, that Satan tempt you not for your incontinency.
6. But I speak this by permission, and not of commandment.
7. For I would that all men were even as I myself. But every man hath his proper gift of God, one after this manner, and another after that.
8. I say therefore to the unmarried and widows: It is good for them if they abide even as I.
9. But if they cannot contain, let them marry; for it is better to marry than to burn.'

It will be seen that in this passage St Paul makes no mention whatever of children: The biological purpose of marriage appears to him wholly unimportant. This is quite natural, since he imagined that the Second Coming was imminent and that the world would soon come to an end. At the Second Coming men were to be divided into sheep and goats, and the only thing of real importance was to find oneself among the sheep on that occasion. St Paul holds that sexual intercourse, even in marriage, is something of a handicap in the attempt to win salvation (1 Cor. viii. 32–34). Nevertheless it is possible for married people to be saved, but fornication is deadly sin, and the unrepentent fornicator is sure to find himself among the goats. I remember once being advised by a doctor to abandon the practice of smoking, and he said that I should find it easier if, whenever the desire came upon me, I proceeded to suck an acid drop. It is in this spirit that St Paul recommends marriage. He does not suggest that it is quite as pleasant as fornication, but he thinks it may enable the weaker brethren to withstand temptation; he does not suggest for a moment that there may be any positive good in marriage, or that affection between husband and wife may be a beautiful and desirable thing, nor does he take the slightest interest in the family; fornication holds the centre of the stage in his thoughts, and the whole of his sexual ethics is arranged with reference to it. It is just as if one were to maintain that the sole reason for baking bread is to prevent people from stealing cake. St Paul does not deign to tell us why he thinks fornication so wicked. One is inclined to suspect that, having thrown over the Mosaic Law, and being therefore at liberty to eat pork, he wishes to show that his morality is neverthelesss quite as severe as that of orthodox Jews. Perhaps the long ages during which pork had been prohibited had made it seem to the Jews as delicious as fornication, and therefore he would need to be emphatic as regards the ascetic elements in his creed.

Condemnation of all fornication was a novelty in the Christian religion. The Old Testament, like most codes of early civilisation, forbids adultery, but it means by adultery intercourse with a married woman. This is evident to anyone who reads the Old Testament attentively. For example, when Abraham goes to Egypt with Sarah he tells the king that Sarah is his sister, and the king, believing this, takes her into his harem; when it subsequently transpires that she is Abraham's wife, the king is shocked to find that he has unwittingly committed sin, and reproaches Abraham for not having told him the facts. This was the usual code of antiquity. A woman who had intercourse outside marriage was thought ill of, but a man was not condemned unless he had intercourse with the wife of another, in which case he was guilty of an offence against property. The Christian view that all intercourse outside marriage is immoral was, as we see in the above passages from St Paul, based upon the view that all sexual intercourse, even within marriage, is regrettable. A view of this sort, which goes against biological facts, can only be regarded by sane people as a morbid aberration. The fact that it is embedded in Christian ethics has made Christianity, throughout its whole history, a force tending towards mental disorders and unwholesome views of life.

St Paul's views were emphasised and exaggerated by the early Church; celibacy was considered holy, and men retired into the desert to wrestle with Satan while he filled their imaginations with lustful visions.

The Church attacked the habit of the bath on the ground that everything that makes the body more attractive tends towards sin. Dirt was praised, and the odour of sanctity became more and more penetrating. 'The purity of the body and its garments,' said St Paula, 'means the impurity of the soul.'[1] Lice were called the pearls of God, and to be covered with them was an indispensable mark of a holy man.

'St Abraham, the hermit, however, who lived for fifty years after his conversion, rigidly refused from that date to wash either his face or his feet. He was, it is said, a person of singular beauty, and his biographer somewhat strangely remarks that 'his face reflected the purity of his soul'. St Ammon had never seen himself naked. A famous virgin, named Silvia, though she was sixty years old, and though bodily sickness was a consequence of her habits, resolutely refused, on religious principles, to wash any part of her body except her fingers. St Euphraxis joined a convent of 130 nuns who never washed their feet, and who shuddered at the mention of a bath. An anchorite once imagined that he was mocked by an illusion of the devil, as he saw gliding before him through the desert a naked creature black with filth and years of exposure, and with white hair floating to the wind. It was a once beautiful woman, St Mary of Egypt, who had thus, during forty-seven years, been expiating her sins. The occasional decadence of the monks into habits of decency was a subject of much reproach. 'Our fathers', said the abbot Alexander, looking mournfully back to the past, 'never washed

[1] Havelock Ellis, *Studies in the Psychology of Sex*, vol. iv, p. 31.

their faces, but we frequent the public baths.' It was related of one monastery in the desert that the monks suffered greatly from want of water to drink; but at the prayer of the abbot Theodosius a copious stream was produced. But soon some monks, tempted by the abundant supply, diverged from their old austerity, and persuaded the abbot to avail himself of the stream for the construction of the bath. The bath was made. Once, and once only, did the monks enjoy their ablutions, when the stream ceased to flow. Prayers, tears, and fastings were in vain. A whole year passed. At last the abbot destroyed the bath, which was the object of the Divine displeasure, and the waters flowed afresh.'[1]

It is evident that, where such views concerning sex prevailed, sexual relations when they occurred would tend to be brutal and harsh, like drinking under Prohibition. The art of love was forgotten and marriage was brutalised.

'The services rendered by the ascetics in imprinting on the minds of men a profound and enduring conviction of the importance of chastity, though extremely great, were seriously counterbalanced by their noxious influence upon marriage. Two or three beautiful descriptions of this institution have been culled out of the immense mass of the patristic writings; but in general, it would be difficult to conceive anything more coarse or more repulsive than the manner in which they regarded it. The relation which nature has designed for the noble purpose of repairing the ravages of death, and which, as Linnaeus has shown, extends even through the world of flowers, was invariably treated as a consequence of the fall of Adam, and marriage was regarded almost exclusively in its lowest aspect. The tender love which it elicits, the holy and beautiful domestic qualities that follow in its train, were almost absolutely omitted from consideration. The

[1] W. E. H. Lecky, *History of European Morals*, vol. ii, pp. 117–18

object of the ascetic was to attract men to a life of virginity, and as a necessary consequence, marriage was treated as an inferior state. It was regarded as being necessary, indeed, and therefore justifiable, for the propagation of the species, and to free men from greater evils; but still as a condition of degradation from which all who aspired to real sanctity could fly. To "cut down by the axe of Virginity the wood of Marriage" was in the energetic language of St Jerome, the end of the saint; and if he consented to praise marriage, it was merely because it produced virgins. Even when the bond had been formed, the ascetic passion retained its sting. We have already seen how it embittered other relations of domestic life. Into this, the holiest of all, it infused a tenfold bitterness. Whenever any strong religious fervour fell upon a husband or a wife, its first effect was to make a happy union impossible. The more religious partner immediately desired to live a life of solitary asceticism, or at least, if no ostensible separation took place, an unnatural life of separation in marriage. The immense place this order of ideas occupies in the hortatory writings of the fathers, and in the legends of the saints, must be familiar to all who have any knowledge of this department of literature. Thus – to give but a very few examples – St Nilus, when he had already two children, was seized with a longing for the prevailing asceticism, and his wife was persuaded, after many tears, to consent to their separation. St Ammon, on the night of his marriage, proceeded to greet his bride with an harangue upon the evils of the married state, and they agreed, in consequence, at once to separate. St Melania laboured long and earnestly to induce her husband to allow her to desert his bed before he would consent. St Abraham ran away from his wife on the night of his marriage. St Alexis, according to a somewhat later legend, took the same step, but many years after returned from Jerusalem to his father's house, in which his wife was still lamenting her desertion, begged and received a lodging as an act of charity, and lived there despised, unrecognised, and unknown till his death.'[1]

The Catholic Church, however, has not remained so un-biological as St Paul and the hermits of the Thebaid. From St Paul one gathers that marriage is to be regarded solely as a more or less legitimate outlet for lust. One would not gather from his words that he would have any objections to birth control; on the contrary, one would be led to suppose that he would regard as dangerous the periods of continence involved in pregnancy and child-birth. The Church has taken a different view. Marriage in the orthodox Christian doctrine has two purposes: one, that recognised by St Paul; the other, the procreation of children. The consequence has been to make sexual morality even more difficult than it was made by St Paul. Not only is sexual intercourse only legitimate within marriage, but even between husband and wife it becomes a sin unless it is hoped that it will lead to pregnancy. The desire for legitimate offspring is, in fact, according to the Catholic Church, the only motive which can justify sexual intercourse. But this motive always justifies it, no matter what cruelty may accompany it. If the wife hates sexual intercourse, if the child is likely to be diseased or insane, if there is not enough money to prevent the utmost extreme of misery, that does not prevent the man from being justified in insisting on his conjugal rights, provided only that he hopes to beget a child.

Catholic teaching on this subject has a twofold basis: it rests, on the one hand, upon the asceticism which we already find in St Paul; on the other, upon the view that it is good to bring into the world as many souls as possible, since every soul is capable of salvation. For some reason which I do not understand, the fact that souls are equally capable of damnation is not taken into account, and yet it seems quite as relevant. Catholics, for example, use their political influence to prevent

[1] W. E. H. Lecky, *History of European Morals*, vol. ii, pp. 339–41.

Protestants from practising birth control, and yet they must hold that the great majority of Protestant children whom their political action causes to exist, will endure eternal torment in the next world. This makes their action seem somewhat unkind, but doubtless these are mysteries which the profane cannot hope to understand.

The recognition of children as one of the purposes of marriage is very partial in Catholic doctrine. It exhausts itself in drawing the inference that intercourse not intended to lead to children is sin. It has never gone so far as to permit the dissolution of a marriage on the ground of sterility. However ardently a man may desire children, if it happens that his wife is barren he has no remedy in Christian ethics. The fact is that the positive purpose of marriage, namely procreation, plays a very subordinate part, and its main purpose remains, as with St Paul, the prevention of sin. Fornication still holds the centre of the stage, and marriage is still regarded essentially as a somewhat less regrettable alternative.

The Catholic Church has tried to cover up this low view of marriage by the doctrine that marriage is a sacrament. The practical efficacy of this doctrine lies in the inference that marriage is indissoluble. No matter what either of the partners may do, if one of them becomes insane or syphilitic or an habitual drunkard, or lives openly with another partner, the relation of the two remains sacred, and although in certain circumstances a separation *a mensa et foro* may be granted, the right to remarry can never be granted. This causes, of course, in many cases a great deal of misery, but since this misery is God's will it must be endured.

Along with this extremely rigid theory, Catholicism has always had a certain degree of toleration for what it held to be sin. The Church has recognised that ordinary human nature could not be expected to live up to its precepts, and has been prepared to give absolution for fornication provided the sinner acknowledged his fault and did penance. This practical toleration was a method of increasing the power of the clergy, since they alone could pronounce absolution, and but for absolution fornication would entail eternal damnation.

The outlook of Protestantism has been somewhat different, in theory less severe, but in practice in some ways more so. Luther was much impressed by the text 'It is better to marry than to burn', and was also in love with a nun. He inferred that, in spite of vows of celibacy, he and the nun had a right to marry, since otherwise, given the strength of his passions, he would have been led into mortal sin. Protestantism accordingly abandoned the praise of celibacy, which had been characteristic of the Catholic Church, and wherever it was vigorous it also abandoned the doctrine that marriage is a sacrament, and tolerated divorce in certain circumstances. But Protestants were more shocked than Catholics by fornication, and altogether more rigid in their moral condemnations. The Catholic Church expected a certain amount of sin, and arranged methods for dealing with it; the Protestants, on the contrary, abandoned the Catholic practices of confession and absolution, and left the sinner in a much more hopeless position than he occupies in the Catholic Church. One sees this attitude in both its aspects in modern America, where divorce is exceedingly easy, but adultery is condemned with far more severity than in most Catholic countries.

It is clear that the whole system of Christian ethics, both in the Catholic and the Protestant forms, requires to be re-examined, as far as possible without the preconceptions to which a Christian education predisposes most of us. Emphatic and reiterated assertion, especially during childhood, produces in most people a belief so firm as to have a hold even over the unconscious, and many of us who imagine that our attitude towards orthodoxy is quite emancipated are still, in fact, subconsciously controlled by its teachings. We must ask ourselves quite frankly what led the Church to condemn all fornication. Do we think that it had valid grounds for this

condemnation? Or, if we do not, are there grounds, other than
those adduced by the Church, which ought to lead us to the
same conclusion? The attitude of the early Church was that
there is something essentially impure in the sexual act, although this act must be excused when it is performed after
fulfilling certain preliminary conditions. This attitude in itself
must be regarded as purely superstitious; the reasons which
led to its adoption were presumably those which were considered in the last chapter as liable to cause an anti-sexual
attitude, that is to say, those who first inculcated such a view
must have suffered from a diseased condition of body or
mind, or both. The fact that an opinion has been widely held
is no evidence whatever that it is not utterly absurd; indeed,
in view of the silliness of the majority of mankind, a widespread belief is more likely to be foolish than sensible. The
Pelew Islanders believe that the perforation of the nose is
necessary for winning eternal bliss.[1] Europeans think that
this end is better attained by wetting the head while pro-
nouncing certain words. The belief of the Pelew Islanders is a
superstition; the belief of the Europeans is one of the truths
of our holy religion.

Jeremy Bentham made a table of the springs of action,
where every human desire was named in three parallel
columns, according as men wish to praise it, to blame it, or to
treat it neutrally. Thus we find in one column 'gluttony', and
opposite it, in the next column, 'love of the pleasures of the
social board.' And again, we find in the column giving eu-
logistic names to impulses, 'public spirit', and opposite to it,
in the next column, we find 'spite'. I recommend anybody
who wishes to think clearly on any ethical topic to imitate
Bentham in this particular, and after accustoming himself to
the fact that almost every word conveying blame has a synonym conveying praise, to acquire a habit of using words that
convey neither praise nor blame. Both 'adultery' and 'for-

[1] Westermarck, *op. cit.,* p. 170.

nication' are words conveying such immensely strong moral reprobation that so long as they are employed it is difficult to think clearly. There are, however, other words used by those lascivious writers who wish to corrupt our morals: such writers will speak of 'gallantry', or 'love unfettered by the cold bonds of law.' Both sets of terms are designed to arouse prejudices; if we wish to think dispassionately, we must eschew the one set just as much as the other. Unfortunately this must inevitably ruin our literary style. Both words of praise and words of blame are colourful and interesting. The reader can be carried along by an invective or panegyric, and with a little skill his emotions can be aroused by the author in any desired direction. We, however, wish to appeal to reason, and we must therefore employ dull neutral phrases, such as 'extra-marital sexual relations'. Yet perhaps this is too austere a precept, for after all we are dealing with a matter in which human emotions are very strongly involved, and if we eliminate emotion too completely from our writing, we may fail to convey the nature of the subject-matter with which we are dealing. In regard to all sexual matters there is a polarity according as they are described from the point of view of the participants or from that of jealous outsiders. What we do ourselves is 'gallantry'; what others do is 'fornication'. We must therefore remember the emotionally coloured terms, and we may employ them on occasion; but we must do so sparingly, and, in the main, we must content ourselves with neutral and scientifically accurate phraseology.

The Christian ethics inevitably, through the emphasis laid upon sexual virtue, did a great deal to degrade the position of women. Since the moralists were men, woman appeared as the temptress; if they had been women, man would have had this role. Since woman was the temptress, it was desirable to curtail her opportunities for leading men into temptation; consequently respectable women were more hedged about with restrictions, while the woman who were not respectable,

being regarded as sinful, were treated with the utmost con-
tumely. It is only in quite modern times that women have
regained the degree of freedom which they enjoyed in the
Roman Empire. The patriarchal system, as we saw, did much
to enslave women, but a great deal of this was undone just
before the rise of Christianity. After Constantine, women's
freedom was again curtailed under the pretence of protecting
them from sin. It is only with the decay of the notion of sin in
modern times that women have begun to regain their freedom.

The writings of the Fathers are full of invectives against
Woman.

'Woman was represented as the door of hell, as the mother of
all human ills. She should be ashamed at the very thought that
she is a woman. She should live in continual penance, on
account of the curses she has brought upon the world. She
should be ashamed of her dress, for it is the memorial of her
fall. She should be especially ashamed of her beauty, for it is
the most potent instrument of the daemon. Physical beauty
was indeed perpetually the theme of ecclesiastical denunci-
ations, though one singular exception seems to have been
made; for it has been observed that in the Middle Ages the
personal beauty of bishops was continually noticed upon their
tombs. Women were even forbidden by a provincial Council,
in the sixth century, on account of their impurity, to receive
the Eucharist into their naked hands. Their essentially subordinate position was continually maintained.'[1]

The laws of property and inheritance were altered in the
same sense against women, and it was only through the free-
thinkers of the French Revolution that daughters recovered
their rights of inheritance.

[1] W. E. H. Lecky, *History of European Morals*, vol. ii, pp. 357–8.

Chapter 6

Romantic Love

With the victory of Christianity and the barbarians, the relations of men and women sank to a pitch of brutality which had been unknown in the ancient world for many centuries. The ancient world was vicious, but not brutal. In the Dark Ages, religion and barbarism combined to degrade the sexual side of life. In marriage, the wife had no rights; outside marriage, since all was sin, there was no object in curbing the natural beastliness of the uncivilised male. The immorality of the Middle Ages was widespread and disgusting; bishops lived in open sin with their own daughters, and archbishops promoted their male favourites to neighbouring sees.[1] There was a growing belief in the celibacy of the clergy, but practice did not keep pace with precept. Pope Gregory VII made immense exertions to cause priests to put away their concubines, yet so late as the time of Abélard we find him regarding it as possible, though scandalous, for him to marry Héloïse. It was only towards the end of the thirteenth century that the celibacy of the clergy was rigidly enforced. The clergy, of course, continued to have illicit relations with women, though they could not give any dignity or beauty to these relations owing to the fact that they themselves considered them immoral and impure. Nor could the Church, in view of its ascetic outlook on sex, do anything whatever to beautify the conception of love. To do this was necessarily the work of the laity.

'It was not surprising that, having once broken their vows and begun to live what they deemed a life of habitual sin, the

[1] Cf. Lea, *History of the Inquisition in the Middle Ages*, vol. i pp. 9, 14.

clergy should soon have sunk far below the level of the laity.
We may not lay much stress on such isolated instances of
depravity as that of Pope John XXIII, who was condemned
for incest, among many other crimes, and for adultery; or the
abbot-elect of St Augustine, at Canterbury, who in 1171 was
found, on investigation, to have seventeen illegitimate children in a single village; or an abbot of St Pelayo, in Spain, who
in 1130 was proved to have kept not less than seventy concubines; or Henry III, Bishop of Liége, who was deposed in
1274 for having sixty-five illegitimate children; but it is impossible to resist the evidence of a long chain of Councils and
ecclesiastical writers, who conspire in depicting far greater
evils than simple concubinage. It was observed that when the
priests actually took wives, the knowledge that these con-
nections were illegal was peculiarly fatal to their fidelity, and
bigamy and extreme mobility of attachments were especially
common among them. The writers of the Middle Ages are
full of accounts of nunneries that were like brothels, of the
vast multitude of infanticides within their walls, and of that
inveterate prevalence of incest among the clergy, which rendered it necessary again and again to issue the most stringent
enactments that priests should not be permitted to live with
their mothers or sisters. Unnatural love, which it had been
one of the great services of Christianity almost to eradicate
from the world, is more than once spoken of as lingering in
the monasteries; and shortly before the Reformation, com-
plaints became loud and frequent of the employment of the
confessional for the purposes of debauchery.'[1]

Throughout the Middle Ages there is the most curious
division between the Greco-Roman traditions of the Church
and the Teutonic traditions of the aristocracy. Each had its
contribution to make towards civilisation, but the con-
tributions were entirely distinct. The Church contributed

[1] W. E. H. Lecky, *History of European Morals*, vol. ii, pp. 350, 351.

learning, philosophy, the canon law, the conception of the unity of Christendom – all of them results of the tradition handed down from Mediterranean antiquity. The laity contributed the common law, the forms of secular government, chivalry, poetry, and romance. The contribution which especially concerns us is romantic love.

To say that romantic love was unknown before the Middle Ages would not be correct, but it was only in the Middle Ages that it became a commonly recognised form of passion. The essential of romantic love is that it regards the beloved object as very difficult to possess and as very precious. It makes therefore great efforts of many kinds to win the love of the beloved object, by poetry, by song, by feats of arms, or by whatever other method may be thought most pleasing to the lady. The belief in the immense value of the lady is a psychological effect of the difficulty of obtaining her, and I think it may be laid down that when a man has no difficulty in obtaining a woman, his feeling towards her does not take the form of romantic love. Romantic love, as it appears in the Middle Ages, was not directed, at first, towards women with whom the lover could have either legitimate or illegitimate sexual relations; it was directed towards women of the highest respectability, who were separated from their romantic lovers by insuperable barriers of morality and convention. So thoroughly had the Church performed its task of making men feel sex inherently impure, that it had become impossible to feel any poetic sentiment towards a lady unless she was regarded as unattainable. Accordingly love, if it was to have any beauty, had to be platonic. It is very difficult for the modern to feel in imagination the psychology of the poet lovers in the Middle Ages. They profess ardent devotion without any desire for intimacy, and this seems to a modern so curious that he is apt to regard their love as no more than a literary convention. Doubtless on occasion it was no more than this, and doubtless its literary expression was dominated by con-

ventions. But the love of Dante for Beatrice, as expressed in
the *Vita Nuova*, is certainly not merely conventional; I should
say, on the contrary, that it is an emotion more passionate
than any known to most moderns. The nobler spirits of the
Middle Ages thought ill of this terrestrial life; our human
instincts were to them the products of corruption and original
sin; they hated the body and its lusts; pure joy was to them
only possible in ecstatic contemplation of a kind that seemed
to them free from all sexual alloy. In the sphere of love, this
outlook could not but produce the kind of attitude which we
find in Dante. A man who deeply loved and respected a
woman would find it impossible to associate with her the idea
of sexual intercourse, since all sexual intercourse would be to
him more or less impure; his love would therefore take poetic
and imaginative forms, and would naturally become filled
with symbolism. The effect of all this upon literature was
admirable, as may be seen in the gradual development of love
poetry, from its beginning in the court of the Emperor Frederick II to its flowering in the Renaissance.

One of the best accounts known to me of love in the later
Middle Ages is to be found in Hurizinga's book on *The
Waning of the Middle Ages* (1924).

'When in the twelfth century [he says] unsatisfied desire was
placed by the troubadours of Provence in the centre of the
poetic conception of love, an important turn in the history of
civilisation was effected. Antiquity, too, had sung the
sufferings of love, but it had never conceived them save as the
expectation of happiness or as its pitiful frustration. The sen-
timental point of Pyramus and Thisbe, of Cephalus and
Procris, lies in their tragic end; in the heartrending loss of a
happiness already enjoyed. Courtly poetry, on the other hand,
makes desire itself the essential *motif*, and so creates a conception of love with a negative ground-note. Without giving
up all connection with sensual love, the new poetic ideal was

capable of embracing all kinds of ethical aspirations. Love now became the field where all moral and cultural perfection flowered. Because of his love, the courtly lover is pure and virtuous. The spiritual element dominates more and more till towards the end of the thirteenth century, the *dolce stil nuovo* of Dante and his friends ends by attributing to love the gift of bringing about a state of piety and holy intuition. Here an extreme had been reached. Italian poetry was gradually to find its way back to a less exalted expression of erotic sentiment. Petrarch is divided between the ideal of spiritualised love and the more natural charm of antique models. Soon the artificial system of courtly love is abandoned, and its subtle distinctions will not be revived, when the Platonism of the Renaissance, latent, already, in the courtly conception, gives rise to new forms of erotic poetry with a spiritual tendency.'

In France and Burgundy, however, the development was not quite the same as it had been in Italy, since French aristocratic ideas of love were dominated by the *Romaunt of the Rose*, which dealt with knightly love but did not insist upon its remaining unsatisfied. It was, in fact, a revulsion against the teaching of the Church and a virtually pagan assertion of love's rightful place in life.

'The existence of an upper class whose intellectual and moral notions are enshrined in an *ars amandi* remains a rather exceptional fact in history. In no other epoch did the ideal of civilisation amalgamate to such a degree with that of love. Just as scholasticism represents the grand effort of the medieval spirit to unite all philosophic thought in a single centre, so the theory of courtly love, in a less elevated sphere, tends to embrace all that appertains to the noble life. The *Roman de la Rose* did not destroy the system; it only modified its tendencies and enriched its contents.'[1]

[1] Huizinga, *The Waning of the Middle Ages*, pp. 95–6.

The age was one of extraordinary coarseness, but the kind
of love advocated by the *Romaunt of the Rose*, while not virtuous in the priestly sense, is refined, gallant, and gentle. Such
ideas were, of course, only for the aristocracy; they pre-
supposed not only leisure, but a certain emancipation from ecclesiastical tyranny. Tournaments, in which motives of love
were prominent, were abhorred by the Church, which however was powerless to suppress them; in like manner it could
not suppress the system of knightly love. In our democratic
age we are apt to forget what the world has owed at various
times to aristocracies. Certainly in this matter of the revival of
love the Renaissance could not have been so successful had
the way not been prepared by the romances of chivalry.

In the Renaissance, as a consequence of the revulsion
towards Paganism, love usually ceased to be platonic although
it remained poetic. What the Renaissance thought of the
medieval convention is to be seen in the account of Don Quix-
ote and his Dulcinea. Nevertheless the medieval tradition
remained not without influence; Sydney's *Astrophel and
Stella* is full of it, and Shakespeare's Sonnets to Mr W. H. are
considerably influenced by it. On the whole, however, the
characteristic love poetry of the Renaissance is cheerful and
straightforward.

> Do not mock me in thy bed
> While these cold nights freeze me dead

says an Elizabethan poet. This sentiment, it must be admitted, is straightforward and uninhibited, and by no means platonic. The Renaissance had, however, learnt from the platonic
love of the Middle Ages to employ poetry as a means of
courtship. Cloten in *Cymbeline* is laughed at because he
cannot produce his own love poem but has to hire a penny-a-
liner, who turns out *Hark, hark, the lark* – quite a creditable
effort, one would say. It is curious that before the Middle
Ages, although there had been a good deal of poetry con-

cerned with love, there was very little that was directly a part of courtship. There is Chinese poetry representing the grief of a lady because of the absence of her lord; there is mystical Indian poetry, in which the soul is represented as the bride longing for the advent of the bridegroom, who is God; but one gathers that *men* had so little difficulty in securing the women they desired that it hardly ever became necessary to woo them with music and poetry. From the point of view of the arts, it is certainly regrettable when women are too accessible; what is most to be desired is that they should be difficult but not impossible of access. This situation has existed more or less since the Renaissance. The difficulties have been partly external and partly internal, the latter being derived from scruples due to conventional moral teaching.

Romantic love reached its apogee in the romantic movement, and one may perhaps take Shelley as its chief apostle. Shelley when he fell in love was filled with exquisite emotions and imaginative thoughts of a kind lending themselves to expression in poetry; naturally enough, he considered that the emotion that produced these results was wholly good, and he saw no reason why love should ever be restrained. His argument, however, rested upon bad psychology. It was the obstacles to his desires that led him to write poetry. If the noble and unfortunate lady Emilia Viviani had not been carried off to a convent, he would not have found it necessary to write *Epipsychidion*; if Jane Williams had not been a fairly virtuous wife, he would never have written *The Recollection*. The social barriers against which he inveighed were an essential part of the stimulus to his best activities. Romantic love as it existed in Shelley depends upon a state of unstable equilibrium, where the conventional barriers still exist but are not quite insuperable; if the barriers are rigid, or if they do not exist, romantic love is not likely to flourish. Take as the one extreme the Chinese system: in this system a man never meets any respectable woman except his own wife, and when he feels her insufficient, he goes to a brothel; his wife is chosen for him and is probably unknown to him until the wedding day; consequently all his sex relations are entirely divorced from love in the romantic sense, and he never has occasion for those efforts of courtship which give rise to love poetry. In a state of complete freedom, on the other hand, a man capable of great love poetry is likely to have so much success through his charm that he will seldom have need of his best imaginative efforts in order to achieve a conquest. Thus love poetry depends upon a certain delicate balance between convention and freedom, and is not likely to exist in its best form where this balance is upset in either direction.

Love poetry, however, is not the only purpose of love, and romantic love may flourish even where it does not lead to artistic expression. I believe myself that romantic love is the source of the most intense delights that life has to offer. In the relation of a man and woman who love each other with passion and imagination and tenderness, there is something of inestimable value, to be ignorant of which is a great misfortune to any human being. I think it important that a social system should be such as to permit this joy, although it can only be an ingredient in life and not its main purpose.

In quite modern times, that is to say, since about the period of the French Revolution, an idea has grown up that marriage should be the outcome of romantic love. Most moderns, at any rate in English-speaking countries, take this for granted, and have no idea that not long ago it was a revolutionary innovation. The novels and plays of a hundred years ago deal largely with the struggle of the younger generation to establish this new basis for marriage as opposed to the traditional marriage of parental choice. Whether the effect has been as good as the innovators hoped may be doubted. There is something to be said for Mrs Malaprop's principle, that love and aversion both wear off in matrimony, so that it is better to begin with a little aversion. Certain it is that when people marry without previous sexual knowledge of each other and under the influence of romantic love, each imagines the other to be possessed of more than mortal perfections and conceives that marriage is going to be one long dream of bliss. This is especially liable to be the case with the woman if she has been brought up ignorant and pure, and therefore incapable of distinguishing sex hunger from congeniality. In America, where the romantic view of marriage has been taken more seriously than anywhere else, and where law and custom alike are based upon the dreams of spinsters, the result has been an extreme prevalence of divorce and an extreme rarity of happy marriages. Marriage is something more serious than the pleasure of two people in each other's company; it is an institution which, through the fact that it gives rise to children, forms part of the intimate texture of society, and has an importance extending far beyond the personal feelings of the husband and the wife. It may be good—I think it is good—that romantic love should form the motive for a marriage, but it should be understood that the kind of love which will enable a marriage to remain happy and to fulfil its social purpose is not romantic, but is something more intimate, affectionate and realistic. In romantic love the beloved object is not seen accurately, but through a glamorous mist. Undoubtedly it is possible for a certain type of woman to remain wrapped in this mist even after marriage, provided she has a husband of a certain type; but this can only be achieved if she avoids all real intimacy with her husband and preserves a sphinx-like secrecy as to her inmost thoughts and feelings, as well as a certain degree of bodily privacy. Such manoeuvres, however, prevent a marriage from realising its best possibilities, which depend upon an affectionate intimacy quite unmixed with illusion. Moreover, the view that romantic love is essential to marriage is too anarchic, and, like St Paul's view, though in an opposite sense, it forgets that children are what makes marriage important. But for children, there would be no need of any institution concerned with sex, but as soon as children enter in, the husband and wife, if they have any offspring, are compelled to realise that their feelings towards each other are no longer what is of most importance.

Chapter 7

The Liberation of Women

The transitional condition of sexual morals at the present time is due in the main to two causes, the first being the invention of contraceptives, and the second the emancipation of women. The former of these causes I shall consider at a later stage; the latter is the subject of this chapter.

The emancipation of women is part of the democratic movement; it begins with the French Revolution, which, as we have already seen, altered the laws of inheritance in a sense favourable to daughters. Mary Wollstonecraft's *Vindication of the Rights of Women* (1792) is a product of the ideas that caused and were caused by the French Revolution. From her time down to the present day the claim of women to equality with men has been asserted with continually increasing emphasis and success. John Stuart Mill's *Subjection of Women* is a very persuasive and well-reasoned book, which had a great influence upon the more thoughtful members of the generation immediately following his own. My father and mother were disciples of his, and my mother used to make speeches in favour of votes for women as early as the 'sixties. So ardent was her feminism that she caused me to be brought into the world by the first woman doctor, Dr Garrett Anderson, who was at that time not allowed to be a qualified medical practitioner but was only a certificated midwife. The feminist movement in those early days was confined to the upper and middle classes, and had therefore not much political strength. A bill to give votes to women came before Parliament every

year, but although always introduced by Mr Faithful Begg
and seconded by Mr Strangways Pigg, it never at that time
had any chance of passing into law. The middle-class feminists of that day had, however, one great success in their own
sphere, namely the passage of the Married Women's Property
Act (1882). Until the passage of that Act, whatever property
a married woman might possess was in her husband's control,
although of course where there was a Trust he could not
spend the capital. The subsequent history of the women's
movement on the political side is too recent and too well
known to need recapitulating. It is, however, worth observing
that the rapidity with which women in most civilised countries have acquired their political rights is without parallel in
the past, considering the immense magnitude of the change in
outlook that has been involved. The abolition of slavery is
more or less analogous, but after all slavery did not exist in
European countries in modern times, and did not concern
anything so intimate as the relations of men and women.

The causes of this sudden change are, I think, twofold: on
the one hand there was the direct influence of democratic
theory, which made it impossible to find any logical answer to
the demands of women; on the other hand there was the fact
that a continually increasing number of women were engaged
in making their own living outside the home, and did not
depend for the comfort of their daily lives upon the favour of
fathers or husbands. This situation, of course, reached its
height during the war, when a very large part of the work
usually performed by men had to be undertaken by women.
Before the war one of the objections commonly urged against
votes for women was that women would tend to be pacifists.
During the war they gave a large-scale refutation of this
charge, and the vote was given to them for their share in the
bloody work. To the idealistic pioneers, who had imagined
that women were going to raise the moral tone of politics,
this issue may have been disappointing, but it seems to be the

fate of idealists to obtain what they have struggled for in a form which destroys their ideals. The rights of women did not, of course, in fact depend upon any belief that women were morally or in any other way superior to men; they depended solely upon their rights as human beings, or rather upon the general argument in favour of democracy. But as always happens when an oppressed class or nation is claiming its rights, advocates sought to strengthen the general argument by the contention that women had peculiar merits, and these merits were generally represented as belonging to the moral order.

The political emancipation of women, however, concerns our theme only indirectly; it is their social emancipation that is important in connection with marriage and morals. In early days, and in the East down to our time, the virtue of women was secured by segregating them. No attempt was made to give them inward self-control, but everything was done to take away all opportunity for sin. In the West this method was never adopted wholeheartedly, but respectable women were educated from their earliest years so as to have a horror of sexual intercourse outside marriage. As the methods of this education became more and more perfected, the outward barriers were more and more removed. Those who did most to remove the outward barriers were convinced that the inward barriers would be sufficient. It was thought, for example, that the chaperon was unnecessary, since a nice girl who had been well brought up would never yield to the advances of young men, whatever opportunities of yielding might be allowed her. It was generally held by respectable women when I was young that sexual intercourse was displeasing to the great majority of women, and was only endured within marriage from a sense of duty; holding this view, they were not unwilling to risk a greater degree of freedom for their daughters than had seemed wise in more realistic ages. The results have perhaps been somewhat different from what was anticipated, and the difference has existed equally as regards wives and as regards unmarried women. The women of the Victorian age were, and a great many women still are, in a mental prison. This prison was not obvious to consciousness, since it consisted of subconscious inhibitions. The decay of inhibitions, which has taken place among the young of our time, has led to the reappearance in consciousness of instinctive desires which had been buried beneath mountains of prudery. This is having a very revolutionary effect upon sexual morality, not only in one country or in one class, but in all civilised countries and in all classes.

The demand for equality between men and women concerned itself from the first not only with political matters but also with sexual morality. The attitude of Mary Wollstonecraft was thoroughly modern, but she was not imitated in this respect by the subsequent pioneers of women's rights. They, on the contrary, were for the most part rigid moralists, whose hope was to impose upon men the moral fetters which hitherto had only been endured by women. Ever since 1914, however, young women, without much theorising, have taken a different line. The emotional excitement of the war was no doubt the precipitating cause of this new departure, but it would have come before very long in any case. The motives of female virtue in the past were chiefly the fear of hell-fire and the fear of pregnancy; the one was removed by the decay of theological orthodoxy, the other by contraceptives. For some time traditional morality managed to hold out through the force of custom and mental inertia, but the shock of the war caused these barriers to fall. Modern feminists are no longer so anxious as the feminists of thirty years ago to curtail the 'vices' of men; they ask rather that what is permitted to men shall be permitted also to them. Their predecessors sought equality in moral slavery, whereas they seek equality in moral freedom.

This whole movement is as yet in a very early phase, and it

is impossible to say how it will develop. Its adherents and practitioners as yet are mostly quite young. They have very few champions among persons of weight and importance. The police, the law, the Church and their parents are against them whenever the facts come to the knowledge of these repositories of power, but in general the young have the kindness to conceal the facts from those to whom they would cause pain. Writers who, like Judge Lindsey, proclaim the facts are thought by the old to be libelling the young, though the young remain unconscious of being libelled.

A situation of this sort is, of course, very unstable. It is a question which of two things will happen first: either the old will become aware of the facts and will set to work to deprive the young of their new-won freedom, or the young, growing up, will themselves acquire positions of dignity and importance, which will make it possible to give the sanction of authority to the new morality. It is to be presumed that in some countries we shall see one of these issues, and in others, the other. In Italy, where immorality, like everything else, is a prerogative of the Government, a vigorous attempt is being made to enforce 'virtue'. In Russia the exact opposite is the case, since the Government is on the side of the new morality. In the Protestant parts of Germany freedom may be expected to win, while in the Catholic parts the issue is much more doubtful. France is hardly likely to be shaken out of the time-honoured French convention in which immorality has certain definitely tolerated forms outside which it must not go. What will happen in England and America, I do not venture to prophesy.

Let us, however, pause a moment to consider the logical implications of the demand that women should be the equals of men. Men have from time immemorial been allowed in practice, if not in theory, to indulge in illicit sexual relations. It has not been expected of a man that he should be a virgin on entering marriage, and even after marriage, infidelities are not viewed very gravely if they never come to the knowledge of a man's wife and neighbours. The possibility of this system has depended upon prostitution. This institution, however, is one which it is difficult for a modern to defend, and few will suggest that women should acquire the same rights as men through the establishment of a class of male prostitutes for the satisfaction of women who wish, like their husbands, to seem virtuous without being so. Yet it is quite certain that in these days of late marriage only a small percentage of men will remain continent until they can afford to set up house with a woman of their own class. And if unmarried men are not going to be continent, unmarried women, on the ground of equal rights, will claim that they also need not be continent. To the moralists this situation is no doubt regrettable. Every conventional moralist who takes the trouble to think it out will see that he is committed in practice to what is called the double standard, that is to say, the view that sexual virtue is more essential in a woman than in a man. It is all very well to argue that his theoretical ethic demands continence of men also. To this there is the obvious retort that the demand cannot be enforced on the men since it is easy for them to sin secretly. The conventional moralist is thus committed against his will not only to an inequality as between men and women, but also to the view that it is better for a young man to have intercourse with prostitutes than with girls of his own class, in spite of the fact that with the latter, though not with the former, his relations are not mercenary and may be affectionate and altogether delightful. Moralists, of course, do not think out the consequences of advocating a morality which they know will not be obeyed; they think that so long as they do not advocate prostitution, they are not responsible for the fact that prostitution is the inevitable outcome of their teaching. This, however, is only another illustration of the well-known fact that the professional moralist in our day is a man of less than average intelligence.

In view of the above circumstances, it is evident that so long as many men for economic reasons find early marriage impossible, while many women cannot marry at all, equality as between men and women demands a relaxation in the traditional standards of feminine virtue. If men are allowed pre-nuptial intercourse (as in fact they are), women must be allowed it also. And in all countries where there is an excess of women it is an obvious injustice that those women who by arithmetical necessity must remain unmarried should be wholly debarred from sexual experience. Doubtless the pioneers of the women's movement had no such consequences in view, but their modern followers perceive them clearly, and whoever opposes these deductions must face the fact that he or she is not in favour of justice to the female sex.

A very clear-cut issue is raised by this question of the new morality versus the old. If the chastity of girls and the faithfulness of wives are no longer to be demanded, it becomes necessary either to have new methods of safeguarding the family or else to acquiesce in the break-up of the family. It may be suggested that the procreation of children should only occur within marriage, and that all extra-marital sexual intercourse should be rendered sterile by the use of contraceptives. In that case husbands might learn to be as tolerant of lovers as Orientals are of eunuchs. The difficulty of such a scheme, as yet, is that it requires us to place more reliance on the efficacy of contraceptives and the truthfulness of wives than seems rational; this difficulty may, however, be diminished with time. The other alternative compatible with the new morality is the decay of fatherhood as an important social institution, and the taking over of the duties of the father by the State. In particular cases where a man felt sure of his paternity and fond of his child, he might, of course, voluntarily undertake to do what fathers now normally do in the way of financial support for the mother and child; but he would not be obliged to do so by law. Indeed all children would be in the position in which illegitimate children of unknown paternity are now, except that the State, regarding this as the normal case, would take more trouble with their nurture than it does at present.

If, on the other hand, the old morality is to be re-established, certain things are essential; some of them are already done, but experience shows that these alone are not effective. The first essential is that the education of girls should be such as to make them stupid and superstitious and ignorant; this requisite is already fulfilled in schools over which the Churches have any control. The next requisite is a very severe censorship upon all books giving information on sex subjects; this condition also is coming to be fulfilled in England and in America, since the censorship, without change of the law, is being tightened up by the increasing zeal of the police. These conditions, however, since they exist already, are clearly insufficient. The only thing that will suffice is to remove from young women all opportunity of being alone with men: girls must be forbidden to earn their living by work outside the home; they must never be allowed an outing unless accompanied by their mother or an aunt; the regrettable practice of going to dances without a chaperon must be sternly stamped out. It must be illegal for an unmarried woman under fifty to possess a motor-car, and perhaps it would be wise to subject all unmarried women once a month to medical examination by police doctors, and to send to a penitentiary all such as were found to be not virgins. The use of contraceptives must, of course, be eradicated, and it must be illegal in conversation with unmarried women to throw doubt upon the dogma of eternal damnation. These measures, if carried out vigorously for a hundred years or more, may perhaps do something to stem the rising tide of immorality. I think, however, that in order to avoid the risk of certain abuses, it would be necessary that all policemen and all medical men should be castrated. Perhaps it would be wise to carry this policy a step farther, in view of the inherent depravity of the male character. I am inclined to think that moralists would be well advised to advocate that all men should be castrated, with the exception of ministers of religion.[1]

It will be seen that there are difficulties and objections whichever course we adopt. If we are to allow the new morality to take its course, it is bound to go farther than it has done, and to raise difficulties hardly as yet appreciated. If, on the other hand, we attempt in the modern world to enforce restrictions which were possible in a former age, we are led into an impossible stringency of regulations, against which human nature would soon rebel. This is so clear that, whatever the dangers or difficulties, we must be content to let the world go forward rather than back. For this purpose we shall need a genuinely new morality. I mean by this that obligations and duties will still have to be recognised, though they may be very different from the obligations and duties recognised in the past. So long as all the moralists content themselves with preaching a return to a system which is as dead as the dodo, they can do nothing whatever to moralise the new freedom or to point out the new duties which it brings with it. I do not think that the new system, any more than the old, should involve unbridled yielding to impulse, but I think the occasions for restraining impulse and the motives for doing so will have to be different from what they have been in the past. In fact the whole problem of sexual morality needs thinking out afresh. The following pages are intended as a contribution, however humble, to this task.

[1] Since reading *Elmer Gantry*, I have begun to feel that even this exception is perhaps not quite wise.

Chapter 8

The Taboo on Sex Knowledge

In the attempt to build up a new sexual morality, the first question we have to ask ourselves is not, how should the relations of the sexes be regulated, but, is it good that men, women, and children should be kept in artificial ignorance of facts relating to sexual affairs? My reason for putting this question first is that, as I shall try to persuade the reader in this chapter, ignorance on such matters is extra-ordinarily harmful to the individual, and therefore no system whose perpetuation demands such ignorance can be desirable. Sexual morality, I should say, must be such as to commend itself to well-informed persons and not to depend upon ignorance for its appeal. This is part of a wider doctrine which, though it has never been held by Governments or policemen, appears indubitable in the light of reason. That doctrine is that right conduct can never, except by some rare accident, be promoted by ignorance or hindered by knowledge. It is, of course, true that if A desires B to act in a certain manner which is in A's interest but not in B's, it may be useful to A to keep B in ignorance of facts which would show B where his true interest lies. This fact is well understood on the Stock Exchange, but is not generally held to belong to the higher departments of ethics. It covers a large part of Governmental activity in concealing facts – for example, the desire which every Government feels to prevent all mention of a defeat in war, for the knowledge of a defeat may lead to the downfall of the Government, which, though usually in the national interest, is, of course, not in the interest of the Government. Reticence about sexual facts, though it belongs in the main to a different department, has had its origin, at least in part, in a similar motive. It was at first only females who were to be kept ignorant, and their ignorance was desired as a help towards masculine domination. Gradually, however, women acquiesced in the view that ignorance is essential to virtue, and partly through their influence it came to be thought that children and young people, whether male or female, should be as ignorant as possible on sexual subjects. At this stage the motive ceased to be one of domination and passed into the region of irrational taboo. The question whether ignorance is desirable is never examined, and it is even illegal to bring evidence to show that ignorance does harm. I may take, as my text on this subject, the following extract from the *Manchester Guardian* of April 25, 1929:

'American Liberals are shocked by the outcome of the court trial of Mrs Mary Ware Dennett, who was yesterday found guilty by a Federal jury in Brooklyn of sending obscene literature through the mails. Mrs Dennett is the author of a highly praised and widely used pamphlet giving in dignified language the elementary facts of sex for children. She is faced with a possible sentence of five years' imprisonment or a fine of £1,000 or both.

'Mrs Dennett, a well-known social worker, is the mother of two grown-up sons, and originally wrote the pamphlet eleven years ago for their instruction. It was printed in a medical magazine and reprinted in pamphlet form at the request of the editor. It has the endorsement of scores of leading physicians, clergymen, and sociologists, and many thousands of copies have been distributed by the Young Men's and Young Women's Christian Associations. It has even been used in the municipal school system of Bronxville, a fashionable suburb of New York.

'The Federal judge, Warren B. Burrows, from New England, who presided, ruled out all the foregoing facts, and refused to let any of the distinguished educators and physicians who were waiting to testify take their stand or permit the jury to hear endorsements of Mrs Dennett's work by prominent authors. The trial virtually consisted of the reading of the pamphlet aloud to a jury of elderly Brooklyn married men, all of whom have been chosen because they had never read any of the works of H. L. Mencken or Havelock Ellis, a test applied by the prosecuting attorney.

'It seems clear that the New York *World* is correct when it says that if Mrs Dennett's work is not permitted to circulate then there is no hope of putting any plain, honest statement of the facts of sex before young people in America. The case will be the subject of an appeal to a higher court, whose decision will be awaited with the greatest interest.'

It happens that this case is American, but it might just as well have been English, since the law in England is practically the same as in America. It will be seen that the law does not allow a person who gives sex information to the young to bring the evidence of experts to show that sex knowledge is desirable for the young. It will be seen also that where a prosecution of this sort is undertaken, it is open to the prosecution to insist that the jury shall consist entirely of ignorant men who have not read anything that will enable them to judge the case rationally. The law declares bluntly that children and young people must not know the facts of sex, and that the question whether it is good or bad for them to know these facts is entirely irrelevant. Nevertheless, since *we* are not in a law-court, and since the present work is not addressed to children, we may be allowed to argue the question whether the traditional practice of keeping children officially in ignorance is desirable or undesirable.

The traditional course with children was to keep them in as

great a degree of ignorance as parents and teachers could achieve. They never saw their parents naked, and after a very early age (provided housing accommodation was sufficient) they did not see their brothers or sisters of the opposite sex naked. They were told never to touch their sexual organs or to speak about them; all questions concerning sex were met by the word 'Hush, hush' in a shocked tone. They were informed that children were brought by the stork or dug up under a gooseberry-bush. Sooner or later they learnt the facts, usually in a more or less garbled form, from other children, who related them secretly, and, as a result of parental teaching, regarded them as 'dirty'. The children inferred that their father and mother behaved to each other in a way which was nasty and of which they themselves were ashamed, since they took so much trouble to conceal it. They learnt also that they had been systematically deceived by those to whom they had looked for guidance and instruction. Their attitude towards their parents, towards marriage, and towards the opposite sex was thus irrevocably poisoned. Very few men or women who have had a conventional upbringing have learnt to feel decently about sex and marriage. Their education has taught them that deceitfulness and lying are considered virtues by parents and teachers; that sexual relations, even within marriage, are more or less disgusting, and that in propagating the species men are yielding to their animal nature while women are submitting to a painful duty. This attitude has made marriage unsatisfying both to men and to women, and the lack of instinctive satisfaction has turned to cruelty masquerading as morality.

The view of the orthodox moralist[1] on the question of sex knowledge may, I fancy, be fairly stated as follows:—

The sexual impulse is a very powerful one, showing itself in different forms at different stages of development. In

[1] This includes the police and the magistrates, but hardly any modern educators.

infancy it takes the form of a desire to touch and play with certain parts of the body; in later childhood it takes the form of curiosity and love of 'dirty' talk, while in adolescence it begins to take more mature forms. There is no doubt that sexual misconduct is promoted by sexual thoughts, and that the best road to virtue is to keep the young occupied in mind and body with matters wholly unconnected with sex. They must therefore be told nothing whatever about sex; they must as far as possble be prevented from talking about it with each other, and 'grown-ups must pretend that there is no such topic. It is possible by these means to keep a girl in ignorance until the night of her marriage, when it is to be expected that the facts will so shock her as to produce exactly that.attitude towards sex which every sound moralist considers desirable in women. With boys the matter is more difficult, since we cannot hope to keep them completely ignorant beyond the age of eighteen or nineteen at latest. The proper course with them is to tell them that masturbation invariably leads to insanity, while intercourse with prostitutes invariably leads to venereal disease. Neither of these assertions is true, but they are white lies, since they are made in the interests of morality. A boy should also be taught that in no circumstances is conversation on sexual subjects permissible, not even in marriage. This increases the likelihood that when he marries he will give his wife a disgust of sex and thus preserve her from the risk of adultery. Sex outside marriage is sin; sex within marriage is not sin, since it is necessary to the propagation of the human species, but is a disagreeable duty imposed on man as a punishment for the Fall, and to be undertaken in the same spirit in which one submits to a surgical operation. Unfortunately, unless great pains are taken, the sexual act tends to be associated with pleasure, but by sufficient moral care this can be prevented, at any rate in the female. It is held to be illegal in England to state in a cheap publication that a wife can and should derive sexual pleasure from intercourse. I have myself heard a pamphlet condemned as obscene in a court of law on this among other grounds. It is on the above outlook in regard to sex that the attitude of the law, the Church, and the old-fashioned educators of the young is based.

Before considering the effect of this attitude in the realm of sex, I should like to say a few words about its consequences in other directions. The first and gravest consequence, in my opinion, is the hampering of scientific curiosity in the young. Intelligent children wish to know about everything in the world; they ask questions about trains and motor-cars and aeroplanes, about what makes rain and about what makes babies. All these curiosities are to the child on exactly the same level; he is merely following what Pavlov calls the 'What-is-it?' reflex, which is the source of all scientific knowledge. When the child in pursuit of the desire for knowledge learns that this desire in certain directions is considered wicked, his whole impulse of scientific curiosity is checked. He does not at first understand what kinds of curiosity are permissible and what kinds are not: if it is wicked to ask how babies are made, it may, for aught the child can tell, be equally wicked to ask how aeroplanes are made. In any case he is driven to the conclusion that scientific curiosity is a danger-ous impulse, which must not be allowed to remain unchecked. Before seeking to know anything, one must anxiously inquire whether this is a virtuous or a vicious kind of knowledge. And since sexual curiosity is generally very strong until it has become atrophied, the child is led to the conclusion that knowledge which he desires is wicked, while the only virtuous knowledge is such as no human being could possibly desire for example, the multiplication table. The pursuit of know-ledge, which is one of the spontaneous impulses of all healthy children, is thus destroyed, and children are rendered artificially stupid. I do not think it can be denied that women are on the average stupider than men, and I believe this to be largely due to the fact that in youth they are more effectively choked off from the pursuit of sex knowledge.

In addition to this intellectual damage, there is in most cases a very grave moral damage. As Freud first showed, and as everyone intimate with children soon discovers, the fables about the stork and the gooseberry-bush are usually disbelieved. The child thus comes to the conclusion that parents are apt to lie to him. If they lie in one matter, they may lie in another, so that their moral and intellectual authority is destroyed. Moreover, since parents lie where sex is concerned, the children conclude that they also may lie on such topics. They talk with each other about them, and very likely they practise masturbation in secret. In this way they learn to acquire habits of deceit and concealment, while, owing to their parents' threats, their lives become clouded with fear. The threats of parents and nurses as to the bad consequences of masturbation have been shown by psycho-analysis to be a very frequent cause of nervous disorders, not only in childhood but in adult life also.

The effects of the conventional treatment of sex in dealing with the young are therefore to make people stupid, deceitful, and timorous, and to drive a not inconsiderable percentage over the border-line into insanity or something like it.

To a certain extent these facts are now recognised by all intelligent people who have to deal with the young; they have, however, not yet become known to the law and those who administer it, as is evident from the case quoted at the beginning of this chapter. Thus the situation is at present that every well-informed person who has to deal with children is compelled to choose whether he will break the law or whether he will cause the children under his charge irreparable moral and intellectual damage. It is difficult to change the law, since most elderly men are so perverted that their pleasure in sex depends upon the belief that sex is wicked and nasty. I am afraid no reform can be hoped for until those who are now old or middle-aged have died.

So far we have considered the bad effects of conventional methods outside the sphere of sex; it is time to consider the more definitely sexual aspects of the question. One of the aims of the moralist is undoubtedly to prevent obsession with sexual subjects; such obsession is at present extraordinarly frequent. A former head master of Eton recently asserted that the conversation of schoolboys is almost always either dull or obscene, yet the schoolboys of whom he had experience were those brought up on the most conventional lines. The fact that a mystery is made about sex enormously increases the natural curiosity of the young on the subject. If adults treat sex exactly as they treat any other topic, giving the child answers to all his questions and just as much information as he desires or can understand, the child never arrives at the notion of obscenity, for this notion depends upon the belief that certain topics should not be mentioned. Sexual curiosity, like every other kind, dies down when it is satisfied. Therefore far the best way to prevent young people from being obsessed with sex is to tell them just as much about it as they care to know.

In saying this I am not arguing *a priori*, but on a basis of experience. What I have observed among the children in my school has shown conclusively, to my mind, the correctness of the view that nastiness in children is the result of prudery in adults. My own two children (a boy aged seven, and a girl aged five) have never been taught that there is anything peculiar either about sex or about excretion, and have so far been shielded to the utmost possible extent from all knowledge of the idea of decency, with its correlative, indecency. They have shown a natural and healthy interest in the subject of where babies come from, but not so much as in engines and railways. Nor have they shown any tendency to dwell upon such topics either in the absence or in the presence of grown-up people. With regard to the other children in the school, we have found that if they came to us at the age of two or three, or even four, they developed exactly like our own children; most of those, however, who came to us at the age of six or seven had already been taught to regard anything connected with the sexual organs as improper. They were surprised to find that in the school such matters were spoken of in the same tone of voice as was employed about anything else, and for some time they enjoyed a sense of release in conversations which they felt to be indecent; finding however, that the grown-ups did nothing to check such conversations, they gradually wearied of them, and became nearly as clean-minded as those who had never been taught decency. They now get merely bored when children new to the school attempt to start conversations which they fondly believe to be improper. Thus by letting fresh air on to the subject it has become disinfected, and the noxious germs which it breeds when kept in darkness have been dissipated. I do not believe that it is possible by any other method to get a group of children whose attitude towards subjects usually considered improper is so wholesome and decent.

There is one aspect of this question which has, I think, not been sufficiently realised by those who wish to cleanse sex from the filth with which it has been covered by Christian moralists. The subject of sex has been associated by nature with excretory processes, and so long as these processes are treated with disgust, it is psychologically natural that some portion of this disgust should attach to sex. It is therefore necessary in dealing with children not to be too fastidious as regards the excretory processes. Certain precautions are, of course, necessary for sanitary reasons, but as soon as children can understand, it should be explained that the reason for these precautions is only sanitary and not that there is anything inherently disgusting about the natural functions concerned.

I am not discussing in this chapter what sexual conduct ought to be, but only what ought to be our attitude on the question of sex knowledge. In what has been said hitherto as to the imparting of sex knowledge to the young, I shall, I hope and believe, have had the sympathy of all enlightened modern educators. I come, however, now to a more debatable topic, in which I fear that I may have more difficulty in securing the sympathy of the reader. This is the topic of what is called obscene literature.

In England and America alike the law declares that literature that is deemed obscene may in certain circumstances be destroyed by the authorities, and the author and publisher may be punished. In England the law under which this can be done is Lord Campbell's Act of 1857. This Act states that:

'If upon complaint there is any reason to believe that any obscene books, etc., are kept in any house or other place, for the purpose of sale or distribution, and upon proof that one or more such articles has been sold or distributed in connection with such a place, justices may, upon being satisfied that such articles are of such a character and description that the publication of them would be a misdemeanour and proper to be prosecuted as such, order by special warrant that such articles shall be seized, and after summoning the occupier of the house, the same or other justices may, if they are satisfied that the articles seized are of the character stated in the warrant, and have been kept for the purpose aforesaid, order them to be destroyed.'[1]

The word 'obscene' which occurs in this Act has no precise legal definition. In practice a publication is legally obscene if the magistrate considers it to be so, and he is not obliged to listen to any evidence by experts to show that in this particular case the publication of matter which might otherwise be considered obscene serves some useful purpose. This

[1] See an excellent discussion by Desmond MacCarthy, 'Obscenity and the Law', *Life and Letters*, May 1929.

means to say that any person who writes a novel, or a socio-logical treatise, or a suggestion for reform in the law as it relates to sexual matters, is liable to have his work destroyed if some ignorant elderly man happens to find it disagreeable reading. The consequences of this law are extraordinarily harmful. As is well known, the first volume of Havelock Ellis's *Studies in the Psychology of Sex* was condemned under this law, although fortunately America proved in this instance more liberal.[1] I do not think anybody could suggest that Have-lock Ellis's purpose was an immoral one, and it seems extra-ordinarily unlikely that such a bulky and learned and serious work would have been read by perons who desired merely the thrill of indecency. It is, of course, impossible to treat of such a subject without discussing matters which the ordinary magistrate would not mention before his wife or daughters,. but to prohibit the publication of such a book is to say that serious students are not to be allowed to know the facts in this domain. From a conventional standpoint I imagine that one of the most objectionable features of Havelock Ellis's work is his collection of case histories, which show how extraordinarily unsuccessful existing methods are in producing either virtue or mental health. Such documents provide data for a rational judgement upon existing methods of sex education; the law declares that we are not to be allowed to have such data, and that our judgements in this domain are to continue to be based upon ignorance.

The condemnation of the *Well of Loneliness* has brought into prominence another aspect of the censorship, namely that any treatment of homosexuality in fiction is illegal. There exists a vast mass of knowledge on homosexuality obtained by students in Continental countries, where the law is less ob-scurantist, but this knowledge is not allowed to be dissemi-nated in England either in a learned form or in the form of

[1] Owing to the prosecution of the first volume, the subsequent volumes were not published in England.

imaginative fiction. Homosexuality between men, though not between women, is illegal in England, and it would be very difficult to present any argument for change of the law in this respect which would not itself be illegal on the ground of obscenity. And yet every person who has taken the trouble to study the subject knows that this law is the effect of a barborous and ignorant superstition, in favour of which no rational argument of any sort or kind can be advanced. Similar considerations apply to incest; not many years ago a new law was passed making certain forms of incest criminal, but it was and is illegal under Lord Campbell's Act to advance arguments either for or against this law, unless such arguments are framed so abstractly and so carefully as to lose all force.

Another interesting consequence of Lord Campbell's Act is that many subjects can be discussed in long technical words known only to highly educated people, which cannot be mentioned in any language understanded of the people. It is permissible with certain precaution to speak in print of *coitus*, but it is not permissible to employ the monosyllabic synonym for this word. This has recently been decided in the case of *Sleeveless Errand*. Sometimes this prohibition of simple language has grave consequences; for example, Mrs Sanger's pamphlet on birth control, which is addressed to working women, was declared obscene on the ground that working women could understand it. Dr Marie Stopes's books, on the other hand, are not illegal, because their language can only be understood by persons with a certain amount of education. The consequence is that, while it is permissible to teach birth control to the well-to-do, it is criminal to teach it to wage-earners and their wives. I commend this fact to the notice of the Eugenics Society, which is perpetually bewailing the fact that wage-earners breed faster than middle-class people, while carefully abstaining from any attempt to change the state of the law which is the cause of this fact.

Many people will agree that these consequences of the law

against obscene publications are regrettable, but they will nevertheless hold that such a law is necessary. I do not myself believe that it is possible to frame a law against obscenity which will not have these undesirable consequences, and in view of this fact, I should myself be in favour of having no law whatever upon the subject. The argument in favour of this thesis is twofold: on the one hand, that no law can forbid the bad without forbidding the good also, and on the other hand, that publications which are undoubtedly and frankly pornographic would do very little harm if sex education were rational.

As regards the first of these theses, it is abundantly established by the history of the use which has been made of Lord Campbell's Act in England. Lord Campbell's Act, as anyone may discover by reading the debates on it, was directed solely to the suppression of pornography, and it was thought at the time that it had been so drafted as to be incapable of use against other types of literature. This belief, however, was based upon an insufficient appreciation of the cleverness of policemen and the stupidity of magistrates. The whole subject of the censorship has been admirably treated in a book by Morris Ernst and William Seagle.[1] They deal with both British and American experience, and more briefly with what has been done elsewhere. Experience shows, especially in the case of the dramatic censorship in England, that frivolous plays calculated to excite lust easily pass the censor, who does not wish to be thought a prig, while serious plays which raise large issues, such as *Mrs Warren's Profession*, take many years to get past the censor, and a play of transcendent poetical merit like the *The Cenci*, although there is not a word in it that could excite lust even in St Anthony, required one hundred years to overcome the disgust which it raised in the manly bosom of the Lord Chamberlain. We may therefore, basing ourselves on a mass of historical evidence, lay it down

[1] *To the Pure*, Viking Press, 1928.

that the censorship will be used against works of serious artistic or scientific merit, while persons whose purpose is purely salacious will always find ways of slipping through the meshes of the law.

There is, however, a further ground for objecting to censorship, and this is that even frank pornography would do less harm if it were open and unashamed than it does when it is rendered interesting by secrecy and stealth. In spite of the law, nearly every fairly well-to-do man has in adolescence seen indecent photographs, and has been proud of obtaining possession of them because they were difficult to procure. Conventional men are of opinion that such things are extraordinarily injurious to others, although hardly one of them will admit that they have been injurious to himself. Undoubtedly they stir a transient feeling of lust, but in any sexually vigorous male such feelings will be stirred in one way if not in another. The frequency with which a man experiences lust depends upon his own physical condition, whereas the occasions which rouse such feelings in him depend upon the social conventions to which he is accustomed. To an early Victorian man a woman's ankles were sufficient stimulus, whereas a modern man remains unmoved by anything up to the thigh. This is merely a question of fashion in clothing. If nakedness were the fashion, it would cease to excite us, and women would be forced, as they are in certain savage tribes, to adopt clothing as a means of making themselves sexually attractive. Exactly similar considerations apply to literature and pictures: what was exciting in the Victorian age would leave the men of a franker epoch quite unmoved. The more prudes restrict the permissible degree of sexual appeal, the less is required to make such an appeal effective. Nine-tenths of the appeal of pornography is due to the indecent feelings concerning sex which moralists inculcate in the young; the other tenth is physiological, and will occur in one way or another whatever the state of the law may be. On these grounds, although I fear that few will agree with me, I am firmly persuaded that there ought to be no law whatsoever on the subject of obscene publications.

The taboo against nakedness is an obstacle to a decent attitude on the subject of sex. Where young children are concerned, this is now recognised by many people. It is good for children to see each other and their parents naked whenever it so happens naturally. There will be a short period, probably at about three years old, when the child is interested in the differences between his father and his mother, and compares them with the differences between himself and his sister, but this period is soon over, and after this he takes no more interest in nudity than in clothes. So long as parents are unwilling to be seen naked by their children, the children will necessarily have a sense that there is a mystery, and having that sense they will become prurient and indecent. There is only one way to avoid indecency, and that is to avoid mystery.

There are also many important grounds of health in favour of nudity in suitable circumstances, such as out-of-doors in sunny weather. Sunshine on the bare skin has an exceedingly health-giving effect. Moreover anyone who has watched children running about in the open-air without their clothes must have been struck by the fact that they hold themselves much better and move more freely and more gracefully than when they are dressed. The same thing is true of grown-up people. The proper place for nudity is out-of-doors in the sunshine and in the water. If our conventions allowed of this, it would soon cease to make any sexual appeal; we should all hold ourselves better, we should be healthier from the contact of air and sun with the skin, and our standards of beauty would more nearly coincide with standards of health, since they would concern themselves with the body and its carriage, not only with the face. In this respect the practice of the Greeks was to be commended.

Chapter 9

The Place of Love
in Human Life

The prevailing attitude of most communities towards love is curiously twofold: on the one hand, it is the chief theme of poetry, novels, and plays; on the other hand, it is completely ignored by most serious sociologists, and is not considered as one of the desiderata in schemes of economic or political reform. I do not think this attitude justifiable. I regard love as one of the most important things in human life, and I regard any system as bad which interferes unnecessarily with its free development.

Love, when the word is properly used, does not denote any and every relation between the sexes, but only one involving considerable emotion, and a relation which is psychological as well as physical. It may reach any degree of intensity. Such emotions as are expressed in *Tristan und Isolde* are in accordance with the experience of countless men and women. The power of giving artistic expression to the emotion of love is rare, but the emotion itself, at least in Europe, is not. It is much commoner in some societies than in others, and this depends, I think, not upon the nature of the people concerned but upon their conventions and institutions. In China it is rare, and appears in history as a characteristic of bad emperors who are misled by wicked concubines: traditional Chinese culture objected to all strong emotions, and considered that a man should in all circumstances preserve the empire of reason. In this it resembled the early eighteenth century. We, who have behind us the Romantic Movement, the French

Revolution, and the Great War, are conscious that the part of reason in human life is not so dominant as was hoped in the reign of Queen Anne. And reason itself has turned traitor in creating the doctrine of psycho-analysis. The three main extra-rational activities in modern life are religion, war, and love; all these are extra-rational, but love is not anti-rational, that is to say, a reasonable man may reasonably rejoice in its existence. Owing to the causes that we have considered in earlier chapters, there is in the modern world a certain antagonism between religion and love. I do not think this antagonism is unavoidable; it is due only to the fact that the Christian religion, unlike some others, is rooted in asceticism.

In the modern world, however, love has another enemy more dangerous than religion, and that is the gospel of work and economic success. It is generally held, especially in America, that a man should not allow love to interfere with his career, and that if he does, he is silly. But in this as in all human matters a balance is necessary. It would be foolish, though in some cases it might be tragically heroic, to sacrifice career completely for love, but it is equally foolish and in no degree heroic to sacrifice love completely for career. Nevertheless this happens, and happens inevitably, in a society organised on the basis of a universal scramble for money. Consider the life of a typical business man of the present day, especially in America: from the time when he is first grown up he devotes all his best thoughts and all his best energies to financial success; everything else is merely unimportant recreation. In his youth he satisfies his physical needs from time to time with prostitutes: presently he marries, but his interests are totally different from his wife's, and he never becomes really intimate with her. He comes home late and tired from the office; he gets up in the morning before his wife is awake; he spends Sunday playing golf, because exercise is necessary to keep him fit for the money-making struggle. His wife's interests appear to him essentially feminine, and while he approves of them, he makes no attempt to share them. He has no time for illicit love any more than for love in marriage, though he may, of course, occasionally visit a prostitute when he is away from home on business. His wife probably remains sexually cold towards him, which is not to be wondered at, since he never has time to woo her. Subconsciously he is dissatisfied, but he does not know why. He drowns his dissatisfaction mainly in work, but also in other less desirable ways, for example, by the sadistic pleasure to be derived from watching prize-fights or persecuting radicals. His wife, who is equally unsatisfied, finds an outlet in second-rate culture, and in upholding virtue by harrying all those whose lives are generous and free. In this way the lack of sexual satisfaction both in husband and wife turns to hatred of mankind disguised as public spirit and a high moral standard. This unfortunate state of affairs is largely due to a wrong conception of our sexual needs. St Paul apparently thought that the only thing needed in a marriage was opportunity for sexual intercourse, and this view has been on the whole encouraged by the teaching of Christian moralists. Their dislike of sex has blinded them to all the finer aspects of the sexual life, with the result that those who have suffered their teaching in youth go about the world blind to their own best potentialities. Love is something far more than desire for sexual intercourse; it is the principal means of escape from the loneliness which afflicts most men and women throughout the greater part of their lives. There is a deep-seated fear, in most people, of the cold world and the possible cruelty of the herd; there is a longing for affection, which is often concealed by roughness, boorishness or a bullying manner in men, and by nagging and scolding in women. Passionate mutual love while it lasts puts an end to this feeling; it breaks down the hard walls of the ego, producing a new being composed of two in one. Nature did not construct human beings to stand alone, since they cannot fulfil her biological purpose except with the help of another; and civilised people cannot fully satisfy their sexual instinct without love. The instinct is not completely satisfied unless a man's whole being, mental quite as much as physical, enters into the relation. Those who have never known the deep intimacy and the intense companionship of happy mutual love have missed the best thing that life has to give; unconsciously, if not consciously, they feel this, and the resulting disappointment inclines them towards envy, oppression and cruelty. To give due place to passionate love should be therefore a matter which concerns the sociologist, since, if they miss this experience, men and women cannot attain their full stature, and cannot feel towards the rest of the world that kind of generous warmth without which their social activities are pretty sure to be harmful.

Most men and women, given suitable conditions, will feel passionate love at some period of their lives. For the inexperienced, however, it is very difficult to distinguish passionate love from mere attraction; especially is this the case with well-brought-up girls, who have been taught that they could not possibly like to kiss a man unless they loved him. If a girl is expected to be a virgin when she marries, it will very often happen that she is trapped by a transient and trivial sex attraction, which a woman with sexual experience could easily distinguish from love. This has undoubtedly been a frequent cause of unhappy marriages. Even where mutual love exists, it may be poisoned by the belief of one or other that it is sinful. This belief may, of course, be well founded. Parnell, for example, undoubtedly sinned in committing adultery, since he thereby postponed the fulfilment of the hopes of Ireland for many years. But even where the sense of sin is unfounded, it will poison love just as much. If love is to bring all the good of which it is capable, it must be free, generous, unrestrained and wholehearted.

The sense of sin which a conventional education attaches to love, even to love within marriage, operates often subconsciously in men as well as in women, and in those whose conscious opinions are emancipated as well as in those who adhere to old traditions. The effects of this attitude are various; it often renders men brutal, clumsy and unsympathetic in their love-making, since they cannot bring themselves to speak about it so as to ascertain the woman's feelings, nor can they adequately value the gradual approaches to the final act which are essential to most women's enjoyment. Indeed they often fail to realise that a woman should experience enjoyment, and that if she does not, her lover is at fault. In women who have been conventionally educated there is often a certain pride in coldness, there is great physical reserve, and an unwillingness to allow easy physical intimacy. A skilful wooer can probably overcome these timidities, but a man who respects and admires them as the mark of a virtuous woman is not likely to overcome them, with the result that even after many years of marriage the relations of husband and wife remain constrained and more or less formal. In the days of our grandfathers, husbands never expected to see their wives naked, and their wives would have been horrified at such a suggestion. This attitude is still commoner than might be thought, and even among those who have advanced beyond this point, a good deal of the old restraint often remains.

There is another more psychological obstacle to the full development of love in the modern world, and that is the fear that many people feel of not preserving their individuality intact. This is a foolish and rather modern terror. Individuality is not an end in itself; it is something that must enter into fructifying contact with the world, and in so doing must lose its separateness. An individuality which is kept in a glass case withers, whereas one that is freely expended in human contacts becomes enriched. Love, children, and work are the great sources of fertilising contact between the individual and the rest of the world. Of these love is usually chronologically the first. Moreover, it is essential to the best development of parental affection, since a child is apt to reproduce the characteristics of both parents, and if they do not love each other, each will only enjoy his own characteristics when they appear in the children, and will be pained by the characteristics of the other parent. Work is by no means always capable of bringing a man into fruitful contact with the outer world. Whether it does so or not depends upon the spirit in which it is undertaken. Work of which the motive is solely pecuniary cannot have this value, but only work which embodies some kind of devotion, whether to persons, to things, or merely to a vision. And love itself is worthless when it is merely possessive; it is then on a level with work which is merely pecuniary. In order to have the kind of value of which we are speaking, love must feel the ego of the beloved person as important as one's own ego, and must realise the other's feelings and wishes as though they were one's own. That is to say, there must be an instinctive and not merely conscious extension of egoistic feeling so as to embrace the other person as well. All this has been rendered difficult by our pugnacious competitive society, and by the foolish cult of personality derived partly from Protestantism and partly from the Romantic Movement.

Among modern emancipated people, love in the serious sense with which we are concerned is suffering a new danger. When people no longer feel any moral barrier against sexual intercourse on every occasion when even a trivial impulse inclines to it, they get into the habit of dissociating sex from serious emotion and from feelings of affection; they may even come to associate it with feelings of hatred. Of this sort of thing Aldous Huxley's novels afford the best illustration. His characters, like St Paul, view sex intercourse merely as a physiological outlet; the higher values with which it is capable of being associated appear to be unknown to them. From such an attitude it is only a step to the revival of asceticism. Love has its own proper ideals and its own intrinsic moral standards. These are obscure both in Christian teaching and in the indiscriminate revolt against all sexual morality which has sprung up among considerable sections of the younger generation. Sex intercourse divorced from love is incapable of bringing any profound satisfaction to instinct. I am not saying that it should never occur, for to ensure this we should have to set up such rigid barriers that love also would become very difficult. What I am saying is that sex intercourse apart from love has little value, and is to be regarded primarily as experimentation with a view to love.

The claims of love to a recognised place in human life, are, as we have seen, very great. But love is an anarchic force which, if it is left free, will not remain within any bounds set by law or custom. So long as children are not involved, this may not greatly matter. But as soon as children appear we are in a different region, where love is no longer autonomous but serves the biological purposes of the race. There has to be a social ethic connected with children, which may, where there is conflict, override the claims of passionate love. A wise ethic will, however, minimise this conflict to the uttermost, not only because love is good in itself, but also because it is food for children when their parents love each other. To secure as little interference with love as is compatible with the interests of children should be one of the main purposes of a wise sexual ethic. This topic, however, cannot be discussed until we have considered the family.

Chapter 10

Marriage

In this chapter I propose to discuss marriage without reference to children, merely as a relation between men and women.
Marriage differs, of course, from other sex relations by the
fact that it is a legal institution. It is also in most communities
a religious institution, but it is the legal aspect which is essential. The legal institution merely embodies a practice which
exists not only among primitive men but among apes and
various other animals. Animals practise what is virtually marriage, wherever the co-operation of the male is necessary to
the rearing of the young. As a rule, animal marriages are
monogamic, and according to some authorities this is the case
in particular amongst the anthropoid apes. It seems, if these
authorities are to be believed, that these fortunate animals are
not faced with the problems that beset human communities,
since the male, once married, ceases to be attracted to any
other female, and the female, once married, ceases to be attractive to any other male. Among the anthropoid apes, therefore, although they do not have the assistance of religion, sin
is unknown, since instinct suffices to produce virtue. There is
some evidence that among the lowest races of savages a similar state of affairs exists. Bushmen are said to be strictly
monogamous, and I understand that the Tasmanians (now
extinct) were invariably faithful to their wives. Even in civilised mankind faint traces of a monogamic instinct can sometimes be perceived. Considering the influence of habit over
behaviour, it is perhaps surprising that the hold of monogamy
on instinct is not stronger than it is. This, however, is an
example of the mental peculiarity of human beings, from

which spring both their vices and their intelligence, namely the power of imagination to break up habits and initiate new lines of conduct.

It seems probable that what first broke up primitive monogamy was the intrusion of the economic motive. This motive, wherever it has any influence upon sexual behaviour, is invariably disastrous, since it substitutes relations of slavery or purchase for relations based upon instinct. In early agricultural and pastoral communities both wives and children were an economic asset to a man. The wives worked for him, and the children, after the age of five or six, began to be useful in the fields or in tending beasts. Consequently the most powerful men aimed at having as many wives as possible. Polygyny can seldom be the general practice of a community, since there is not as a rule a great excess of females; it is the prerogative of chiefs and rich men. Many wives and children form a valuable property, and will therefore enhance the already privileged position of their owners. Thus the primary function of a wife comes to be that of a lucrative domestic animal, and her sexual function becomes subordinated. At this level of civilisation it is as a rule easy for a man to divorce his wife, though he must in that case restore to her family any dowry that she may have brought. It is, however, in general impossible for a wife to divorce her husband.

The attitude of most semi-civilised communities towards adultery is of a piece with this outlook. At a very low level of civilisation adultery is sometimes tolerated. The Samoans, we are told, when they have to go upon a journey, fully expect their wives to console themselves for their absence.[1] At a slightly higher level, however, adultery in women is punished with death or at best with very severe penalties. Mungo Park's account of Mumbo Jumbo used to be well known when I was young, but I have been pained in recent years to find highbrow Americans alluding to Mumbo Jumbo as a god of the

[1] Margaret Mead, *Coming of Age in Samoa*, 1928, pp. 104 ff.

Congo. He was in fact neither a god nor connected with the Congo. He was a pretence demon invented by the men of the Upper Niger to terrify women who had sinned. Mungo Park's account so inevitably suggests a Voltairean view as to the origins of religion that it has tended to be discreetly suppressed by modern anthropologists, who cannot bear the intrusion of rational scoundrelism into the doings of savages. A man who had intercourse with another man's wife was of course also a criminal, but a man who had intercourse with an unmarried woman did not incur any blame unless he diminished her value in the marriage market.

With the coming of Christianity this outlook was changed. The part of religion in marriage was very greatly augmented, and infractions of the marriage law came to be blamed on grounds of taboo rather than of property. To have intercourse with another man's wife remained, of course, an offence against that man, but to have any intercourse outside marriage was an offence against God, and, this, in the view of the Church, was a far graver matter. For the same reason divorce, which had previously been granted to men on easy terms, was declared inadmissible. Marriage became a sacrament and therefore lifelong.

Was this a gain or a loss to human happiness? It is very hard to say. Among peasants the life of married women has always been a very hard one, and on the whole it has been hardest among the least civilised peasants. Among most barbarous peoples a woman is old at twenty-five, and cannot hope at that age to retain any traces of beauty. The view of woman as a domestic animal was no doubt very pleasant for men, but for women it meant a life of nothing but toil and hardship. Christianity, while in some ways it made the position of women worse, especially in the well-to-do classes, did at least recognise their theological equality with men, and refused to regard them as absolutely the property of their husbands. A married woman had not, of course, the right to

leave her husband for another man, but she could leave him
for a life of religion. And on the whole progress towards a
better status for women was easier, in the great bulk of the
population, from the Christian than from the pre-Christian
standpoint.

When we look round the world at the present day and ask
ourselves what conditions seem on the whole to make for
happiness in marriage and what for unhappiness, we are
driven to a somewhat curious conclusion: that the more civilised people become the less capable they seem of lifelong
happiness with one partner. Irish peasants, although until
recent times marriages were decided by the parents, were said
by those who ought to know them to be on the whole happy
and virtuous in their conjugal life. In general, marriage is
easiest where people are least differentiated. When a man
differs little from other men, and a woman differs little from
other women, there is no particular reason to regret not
having married someone else. But people with multifarious
tastes and pursuits and interests will be apt to desire congeniality in their partners, and to feel dissatisfied when they
find that they have secured less of it than they might have
obtained. The Church, which tends to view marriage solely
from the point of view of sex, sees no reason why one partner
should not do just as well as another, and can therefore
uphold the indissolubility of marriage without realising the
hardship that this often involves.

Another condition which makes for happiness in marriage
is paucity of unowned women and absence of social occasions
when married men meet respectable women. If there is no
possibility of sexual relations with any woman other than
one's wife, most men will make the best of the situation, and,
except in abnormally bad cases, will find it quite tolerable.
The same thing applies to wives, especially if they never
imagine that marriage should bring much happiness. That is
to say, a marriage is likely to be what is called happy if

neither party ever expected to get much happiness out of it.

Fixity of social custom, for the same reason, tends to prevent what are called unhappy marriages. If the bonds of marriage are recognised as final and irrevocable, there is no stimulus to the imagination to wander outside and consider that a more ecstatic happiness might have been possible. In order to secure domestic peace where this state of mind exists, it is only necessary that neither the husband nor the wife should fall outragiously below the commonly recognised standard of decent behaviour, whatever this may be.

Among civilised people in the modern world none of these conditions for what is called happiness exist, and accordingly one finds that not many marriages after the first few years are happy. Some of the causes of unhappiness are bound up with civilisation, but others would disappear if men and women were more civilised than they are. Let us begin with the latter. Of these the most important is bad sexual education, which is a far commoner thing among the well-to-do than it can ever be among peasants. Peasant children early become accustomed to what are called the facts of life, which they can observe not only among human beings but among animals. They are thus saved from both ignorance and fastidiousness. The carefully educated children of the well-to-do, on the contrary, are shielded from all practical knowledge of sexual matters, and even the most modern parents, who teach children out of books, do not give them that sense of practical familiarity which the peasant child early acquires. The triumph of Christian teaching is when a man and woman marry without either having had previous sexual experience. In a large proportion of cases where this occurs, the results are unfortunate. Sexual behaviour among human beings is not instinctive, so that the inexperienced bride and bridegroom, who are probably quite unaware of this fact, find themselves overwhelmed with shame and discomfort. It is little better when the woman alone is innocent but the man has acquired

his knowledge from prostitutes. Most men do not realise that
a process of wooing is necessary after marriage, and many
well-brought-up women do not realise what harm they do to
marriage by remaining reserved and physically aloof. All this
could be put right by better sexual education, and is in fact
very much better with the generation now young than it was
with their parents and grandparents. There used to be a widespread belief among women that they were morally superior
to men on the ground that they had less pleasure in sex. This
attitude made frank companionship between husbands and
wives impossible. It was of course in itself quite unjustifiable,
since failure to enjoy sex, so far from being virtuous, is a mere
physiological or psychological deficiency, like a failure to
enjoy food, which also a hundred years ago was expected of
elegant females.

Other modern causes of unhappiness in marriages are,
however, not so easily disposed of. I think that uninhibited
civilised people, whether men or women, are generally poly-
gamous in their instincts. They may fall deeply in love and
be for some years entirely absorbed in one person, but sooner
or later sexual familiarity dulls the edge of passion, and then
they begin to look elsewhere for a revival of the old thrill. It is,
of course, possible to control this impulse in the interests of
morality, but it is very difficult to prevent the impulse from
existing. With the growth of women's freedom there has come
a much greater opportunity for conjugal infidelity than existed in former times. The opportunity gives rise to the
thought, the thought gives rise to the desire, and in the absence of religious scruples the desire gives rise to the act.

Women's emancipation has in various ways made marriage
more difficult. In old days the wife had to adapt herself to the
husband, but the husband did not have to adapt himself to the
wife. Nowadays many wives, on grounds of woman's right to
her own individuality and her own career, are unwilling to
adapt themselves to their husbands beyond a point, while men

who still hanker after the old tradition of masculine domination see no reason why they should do all the adapting. This trouble arises especially in connection with infidelity. In old days the husband was occasionally unfaithful, but as a rule his wife did not know of it. If she did, he confessed that he had sinned and made her believe that he was penitent. She, on the other hand, was usually virtuous. If she was not, and the fact came to her husband's knowledge, the marriage broke up. Where, as happens in many modern marriages, mutual faithfulness is not demanded, the instinct of jealousy nevertheless survives, and often proves fatal to the persistence of any deeply rooted intimacy even where no overt quarrels occur.

There is another difficulty in the way of modern marriage, which is felt especially by those who are most conscious of the value of love. Love can only flourish as long as it is free and spontaneous; it tends to be killed by the thought that it is a duty. To say that it is your duty to love so-and-so is the surest way to cause you to hate him or her. Marriages as a combination of love with legal bonds thus falls between two stools. Shelley says:

> I never was attached to that great sect
> Whose doctrine is that each one should select
> Out of the crowd a mistress or a friend,
> And all the rest, though wise and good, commend
> To cold oblivion; though it is the code
> Of modern morals, and the beaten road
> Which those poor slaves with weary footsteps tread
> Who travel to their home among the dead
> By the broad highway of the world, and so
> With one chain'd friend, perhaps a jealous foe,
> The dreariest and the longest journey go.

There can be no doubt that to close one's mind on marriage against all the approaches of love from elsewhere is to diminish receptivity and sympathy and the opportunities of valuable human contacts. It is to do violence to something which, from the most idealistic standpoint, is in itself desirable. And like every kind of restrictive morality it tends to promote what one may call a policeman's outlook upon the whole of human life – the outlook, that is to say, which is always looking for opportunities to forbid something.

For all these reasons, many of which are bound up with things undoubtedly good, marriage has become difficult, and if it is not to be a barrier to happiness it must be conceived in a somewhat new way. One solution often suggested, and actually tried on a large scale in America, is easy divorce. I hold, of course, as every humane person must, that divorce should be granted on more grounds than are admitted in the English law, but I do not recognise in easy divorce a solution of the troubles of marriage. Where a marriage is childless, divorce may be often the right solution, even when both parties are doing their best to behave decently; but where there are children the stability of marriage is to my mind a matter of considerable importance. (This is a subject to which I shall return in connection with the family.) I think that, where a marriage is fruitful and both parties to it are reasonable and decent, the expectation ought to be that it will be lifelong, but not that it will exclude other sex relations. A marriage which begins with passionate love and leads to children who are desired and loved ought to produce so deep a tie between a man and woman that they will feel something infinitely precious in their companionship, even after sexual passion has decayed, and even if either or both feels sexual passion for someone else. This mellowing of marriage has been prevented by jealousy, but jealousy, though it is an instinctive emotion, is one which can be controlled if it is recognised as bad, and not supposed to be the expression of a just moral indignation. A companionship which has lasted for many years and through many deeply felt events has a richness of content which cannot belong to the first days of love, however delightful these may be. And any person who appreciates what time can do to enhance values will not lightly throw away such companionship for the sake of new love.

It is therefore possible for a civilised man and woman to be happy in marriage, although if this is to be the case a number of conditions must be fulfilled. There must be a feeling of complete equality on both sides; there must be no interference with mutual freedom; there must be the most complete physical and mental intimacy; and there must be a certain similarity in regard to standards of values. (It is fatal, for example, if one values only money while the other values only good work.) Given all these conditions, I believe marriage to be the best and most important relation that can exist between two human beings. If it has not often been realised hitherto, that is chiefly because husbands and wives have regarded themselves as each other's policemen. If marriage is to achieve its possibilities, husbands and wives must learn to understand that whatever the law may say, in their private lives they must be free.

Chapter 11

Prostitution

So long as the virtue of respectable women is regarded as a matter of great importance, the institution of marriage has to be supplemented by another institution which may really be regarded as a part of it – I mean the institution of prostitution. Everybody is familiar with the famous passage in which Lecky speaks of prostitutes as safeguards of the sanctity of the home and of the innocence of our wives and daughters. The sentiment is Victorian, and the manner of expression is old-fashioned, but the fact is undeniable. Moralists have denounced Lecky because his remark made them feel furious and they did not quite know why, but they have not succeeded in showing that what he said was untrue. The moralist asserts, of course quite truly, that if men followed his teaching there would be no prostitution, but he knows quite well that they will not follow it, so that the consideration of what would happen if they did is irrelevant.

The need for prostitution arises from the fact that many men are either unmarried or away from their wives on journeys, that such men are not content to remain continent, and that in a conventionally virtuous community they do not find respectable women available. Society therefore sets apart a certain class of women for the satisfaction of those masculine needs which it is ashamed to acknowledge yet afraid to leave wholly unsatisfied. The prostitute has the advantage, not only that she is available at a moment's notice, but that, having no life outside her profession, she can remain hidden without difficulty, and the man who has been with her can return to his wife, his family, and his church with unimpaired dignity. She, however, poor woman, in spite of the undoubted service she performs, in spite of the fact that she safeguards the virtue of wives and daughters and the apparent virtue of churchwardens, is universally despised, thought to be an out-cast, and not allowed to associate with ordinary people except in the way of business. This blazing injustice began with the victory of the Christian religion, and has been continued ever since. The real offence of the prostitute is that she shows up the hollowness of moralistic professions. Like the thoughts repressed by the Freudian censor, she must be banished into the unconscious. Thence, however, as such exiles will, she wreaks an unintended vengeance.

> But most, through midnight streets I hear
> How the youthful harlot's curse
> Blasts the new-born infants tear
> And blights with plagues the marriage-hearse

Prostitution was not always the despised and hidden thing that it has become. Its origin, indeed, is as lofty as could be. Originally the prostitute was a priestess dedicated to a god or a goddess, and in serving the passing stranger she was per-forming an act of worship. In those days she was treated with respect, and while men used her they honoured her. The Christian Fathers filled many pages with invectives against this system, which, they said, showed the lasciviousness of the Pagan worship and its origin in the wiles of Satan. The temples were closed, and prostitution became everywhere what it had already become in many places, a commercialised institution run for profit – not, of course, for the profit of the prostitutes, but of those whose virtual slaves they were, for until fairly recent times the individual prostitute, who is now the rule, was a rare exception, and the great majority were in brothels or baths or other institutions of ill-fame. In India the transi-tion from religious to commercial prostitution is not yet quite complete. Katherine Mayo, the author of *Mother India*, adduces the survival of religious prostitution as one of the counts of her indictment against that country.

Prostitution, except in South America,[1] appears to be on the decline, partly, no doubt, owing to the fact that other means of livelihood are more available to women than they used to be, and partly also to the fact that many more women than used to be the case are now willing to have extra-marital relations with men, from inclination and not from commercial motives. Nevertheless, I do not think that prostitution can be abolished wholly. Take, for example, sailors when they come ashore after a long voyage. They cannot be expected to have the patience to woo women who will only come to them out of affection. Or take again the fairly large class of men who are unhappy in marriage and afraid of their wives. Such men will seek ease and release when they are away from home, and will desire it in a form as free from psychological obligations as possible. There are, nevertheless, serious reasons for wishing to reduce prostitution to a minimum. It is open to three grave objections: first, the danger to the health of the community; second, the psychological damage to women; and third, the psychological damage to men.

The danger to health is the most important of these three. It is, of course, mainly through prostitutes that venereal disease is spread. The attempts to cope with this problem by registration of prostitutes and State inspection have not been found very successful from a purely medical point of view, and are liable to unpleasant abuses because of the hold which they give to the police over prostitutes, and even on occasion over women who had no intention of becoming professional prostitutes, but have found themselves unintentionally included within the legal definition. Venereal disease could, of course, be coped with much more effectively than it is, if it were not regarded as a just punishment for sin. It is possible to take precautions in advance which much diminish the likelihood of

[1] See Albert Londres, *The Road to Buenos Ayres*, 1929.

it, but it is thought undesirable to make the nature of these precautions widely known, on the ground that such knowledge might promote sin. And those who acquire a venereal disease often postpone treatment because they are ashamed, any disease of this sort being considered disgraceful. The attitude of the community in these respects is undoubtedly better than it used to be, and if it improves still farther, the result may be a very considerable diminution of venereal disease. Nevertheless, it is obvious that prostitution, so long as it exists, will afford a means of spreading disease more dangerous than any other.

Prostitution as it exists at present is obviously an undesirable kind of life. The risk of disease in itself renders prostitution a dangerous trade like working in white lead, but apart from that the life is a demoralising one. It is idle, and tends to excessive drinking. It has the grave drawback that the prostitute is generally despised, and is probably thought ill of even by her clients. It is a life against instinct – quite as much against instinct as the life of a nun. For all these reasons prostitution, as it exists in Christian countries, is an extraordinarily undesirable career.

In Japan, apparently, the matter is quite otherwise. Prostitution is recognised and respected as a career, and is even adopted at the instance of parents. It is even a not uncommon method of earning a marriage dowry. According to some authorities, the Japanese have a partial immunity from syphilis. Accordingly the career of a prostitute in Japan has not the sordidness that it has where morality is more stern. Clearly, if prostitution must survive, it is better that it should exist in the Japanese form than in that to which we are accustomed in Europe. It is obvious that the more strict the standard of morality in any country, the more degradation will attach to the life of a prostitute.

Association with prostitutes, if it becomes at all habitual, is likely to have a bad psychological effect upon a man. He will get into the habit of feeling that it is not necessary to please in order to have sexual intercourse. He will also, if he respects the usual moral code, tend to feel contempt for any woman with whom he has intercourse. The reaction of this state of mind upon marriage may be extraordinarily unfortunate, both where it takes the form of assimilating marriage to prostitution, and where it takes the opposite form of differentiating it as widely as possible. Some men are incapable of desiring sexual intercourse with a woman whom they deeply love and respect. This is attributed by Freudians to the Oedipus complex, but is, I think, quite as often due to the desire to place as wide a gulf as possible between such women and prostitutes. Without going to these extreme lengths, many men, especially old-fashioned men, treat their wives with an exaggerated respect, which leaves them psychologically virginal, and prevents them from experiencing sexual pleasure. Exactly the opposite evils results when a man in imagination assimilates his wife to a prostitute. This leads him to forget that sexual intercourse should only occur when both desire it, and that it should be approached invariably by a period of courtship. He is accordingly rough and brutal with his wife, and produces in her a disgust which it is very difficult to eradicate.

The intrusion of the economic motive into sex is always in a greater or lesser degree disastrous. Sexual relations should be a mutual delight, entered into solely from the spontaneous impulse of both parties. Where this is not the case, everything that is valuable is absent. To use another person in so intimate a manner is to be lacking in that respect for the human being as such, out of which all true morality must spring. To a sensitive person, such an act cannot be in any serious way attractive. If, nevertheless, it is performed from the sheer strength of the physical urge, it is likely to lead to remorse, and in remorse a man's judgments of value are disordered. This applies, of course, not only to prostitution, but almost as much to marriage. Marriage is for women the commonest mode of livelihood, and the total amount of undesired sex endured by women is probably greater in marriage than in prostitution. Morality in sexual relations, when it is free from superstition, consists essentially of respect for the other person, and unwillingness to use that person solely as a means of personal gratification without regard to his or her desires. It is because prostitution sins against this principle that it would remain undesirable even if prostitutes were respected and the risk of venereal disease were eliminated.

Havelock Ellis, in his very interesting study of prostitution, advances an argument in its favour which I do not believe to be valid. He begins by a consideration of the orgy, which exists in most early civilisations, and affords an outlet for anarchic impulses which at other times have to be controlled. According to him, prostitution developed out of the orgy, and serves in some degree the purpose which the orgy formerly served. Many men, he says, cannot find complete satisfaction within the restraints, the decorum, and the decent limitations of a conventional marriage, and such men, he thinks, find in an occasional visit to a prostitute an outlet less antisocial than any other that is open to them. At bottom, however, his argument is the same as Lecky's, although its form is more modern. Women whose sexual life is uninhibited are as liable as men to the impulses which Havelock Ellis is considering, and if the sexual life of women is liberated, men will be able to find satisfaction for the impulses concerned, without having to seek the company of professionals whose motive is purely pecuniary. This is indeed one of the great advantages to be hoped from the sexual liberation of women. As far as I have been able to observe, women whose opinions and feelings about sex are not subject to the old taboos are able to find and give much fuller satisfaction in marriage than was possible in Victorian days. Wherever the older morality has decayed, prostitution also has decayed. The young man who would formerly have been driven to oc-

casional visits to prostitutes is now able to enter upon relations with girls of his own kind, relations which are on both
sides free, which have a psychological element quite as important as the purely physical, and which involve often a
considerable degree of passionate love on both sides. From
the point of view of any genuine morality, this is an immense
advance upon the older system. Moralists regret it because it
is less easy to conceal, but it is after all not the first principle
of morality that lapses from virtue should not come to the ears
of the moralist. The new freedom between young people is, to
my mind, wholly a matter for rejoicing, and is producing a
generation of men without brutality and women without
finicky fastidiousness. Those who oppose the new freedom
should face frankly the fact that they are in effect advocating
the continuance of prostitution as the sole safety-valve against
the pressure of an impossibly rigid code.

Chapter 12

Trial
Marriage

In a rational ethic, marriage would not count as such in the absence of children. A sterile marriage should be easily dissoluble, for it is through children alone that sexual relations become of importance to society, and worthy to be taken cognisance of by a legal institution. This, of course, is not the view of the Church, which, under the influence of St Paul, still views marriage rather as the alternative to fornication than as the means to the procreation of children. In recent years, however, even clergymen have become aware that neither men nor women invariably wait for marriage before experiencing sexual intercourse. In the case of men, provided their lapses were with prostitutes and decently concealed, they were comparatively easy to condone, but in the case of women other than professional prostitutes, the conventional moralists find what they call immorality much harder to put up with. Nevertheless, in America, in England, in Germany, in Scandinavia, a great change has taken place since the war. Very many girls of respectable families have ceased to think it worth while to preserve their 'virtue', and young men, instead of finding an outlet with prostitutes, have had affairs with girls of the kind whom, if they were richer, they would wish to marry. It seems that this process has gone farther in the United States than it has in England, owing, I think, to Prohibition and automobiles. Owing to Prohibition, it has become *de rigueur* at any cheerful party for everybody to get more or less drunk. Owing to the fact that a very large percentage of girls possess cars of their own, it has become easy for them to escape with a lover from the eyes of parents and neighbours. The resulting state of affairs is described in Judge Lindsey's books.[1] The old accuse him of exaggeration, but the young do not. As far as a casual traveller can, I took pains to test his assertions by questioning young men. I did not find them inclined to deny anything that he said as to the facts. It seems to be the case throughout America that a very large percentage of girls who subsequently marry and become of the highest respectability have sex experience, often with several lovers. And even where complete relations do not occur, there is so much 'petting' and 'necking' that the absence of complete intercourse can only be viewed as a perversion.

I cannot say myself that I view the present state of affairs as satisfactory. It has certain undesirable features imposed upon it by conventional moralists, and until conventional morality is changed, I do not see how these undesirable features are to disappear. Bootlegged sex is in fact as inferior to what it might be as bootlegged alcohol. I do not think anybody can deny that there is enormously more drunkenness among young men, and still more among young women, in well-to-do America than there was before the introduction of Prohibition. In circumventing the law there is, of course, a certain spice and a certain pride of cleverness, and while the law about drink is being circumvented it is natural to circumvent the conventions about sex. Here, also, the sense of daring acts as an aphrodisiac. The consequence is that sex relations between young people tend to take the silliest possible form, being entered into not from affection but from bravado, and at times of intoxication. Sex, like liquor, has to be taken in forms which are concentrated and rather unpalatable, since these forms alone can escape the vigilance of the authorities. Sex relations as a dignified, rational, wholehearted activity in which the

[1] *The Revolt of Modern Youth*, 1925. *Companionate Marriage*, 1927.

complete personality co-operates, do not often, I think, occur in America outside marriage. To this extent the moralists have been successful. They have not prevented fornication; on the contrary, if anything, their opposition, by making it spicy, has made it more common. But they have succeeded in making it almost as undesirable as they say it is, just as they have succeeded in making much of the alcohol consumed as poisonous as they assert all alcohol to be. They have compelled young people to take sex neat, divorced from daily companionship, from a common work, and from all psychological intimacy. The more timid of the young do not go so far as complete sexual relations, but content themselves with producing prolonged states of sexual excitement without satisfaction, which are nervously debilitating, and calculated to make the full enjoyment of sex at a later date difficult or impossible. Another drawback to the type of sexual excitement which prevails among the young in America is that it involves either failure to work or loss of sleep, since it is necessarily connected with parties which continue into the small hours.

A graver matter, while official morality remains what it is, is the risk of occasional disaster. By ill luck it may happen that some one young person's doings come to the ears of some guardian of morality, who will proceed with a good conscience to a sadistic orgy of scandal. And since it is almost impossible for young people in America to acquire a sound knowledge of birth-control methods, unintended pregnancies are not infrequent. These are generally dealt with by procuring abortion, which is dangerous, painful, illegal, and by no means easy to keep secret. The complete gulf between the morals of the young and the morals of the old, which exists very commonly in present-day America, has another unfortunate result, namely that often there can be no real intimacy or friendship between parents and children, and that the parents are incapable of helping their children with advice or sympathy.

When young people get into a difficulty, they cannot speak of it to their parents without producing an explosion – possibly scandal, certainly a hysterical upheaval. The relation of parent and child has thus ceased to be one performing any useful function after the child has reached adolescence. How much more civilised are the Trobriand Islanders, where a father will say to his daughter's lover: 'You sleep with my child: very well, marry her.'[1]

In spite of the drawbacks we have been considering, there are great advantages in the emancipation, however partial, of young people in America, as compared with their elders. They are freer from priggery, less inhibited, less enslaved to authority devoid of rational foundation. I think also that they are likely to prove less cruel, less brutal, and less violent than their seniors. For it has been characteristic of American life to take out in violence the anarchic impulses which could not find an outlet in sex. It may also be hoped that when the generation now young reaches middle age, it will not wholly forget its behaviour in youth, and will be tolerant of sexual experiments which at present are scarcely possible because of the need of secrecy.

The state of affairs in England is more or less similar to that in America, though not so developed owing to the absence of Prohibition and the paucity of motor-cars. There is also, I think, in England, and certainly on the Continent, very much less of the practice of sexual excitement without ultimate satisfaction. And respectable people in England, with some honourable exceptions, are on the whole less filled with persecuting zeal than corresponding people in America. Nevertheless, the difference between the two countries is only one of degree.

Judge Ben B. Lindsey, who was for many years in charge of the juvenile court at Denver, and in that position had unrivalled opportunities for ascertaining the facts, proposed a

[1] Malinowski, *The Sexual Life of Savages*, p. 73.

new institution which he calls 'companionate marriage'. Unfortunately he has lost his official position, for when it became known that he used it rather to promote the happiness of the young than to give them a consciousness of sin, the Ku Klux Klan and the Catholics combined to oust him. Companionate marriage is the proposal of a wise conservative. It is an attempt to introduce some stability into the sexual relations of the young, in place of the present promiscuity. He points out the obvious fact that what prevents the young from marrying is lack of money, and that money is required in marriage partly on account of children, but partly also because it is not the thing for the wife to earn her own living. His view is that young people should be able to enter upon a new kind of marriage, distinguished from ordinary marriage by three characteristics. First, that there should be for the time being no intention of having children, and that accordingly the best available birth-control information should be given to the young couple. Second, that so long as there are no children and the wife is not pregnant, divorce should be possible by mutual consent. And third, that in the event of divorce, the wife should not be entitled to alimony. He holds, and I think rightly, that if such an institution were established by law, a very great many young people, for example students at universities, would enter upon comparatively permanent partnerships, involving a common life, and free from the Dionysiac characteristics of their present sex relations. He brings evidence to bear that young students who are married do better work than such as are unmarried. It is indeed obvious that work and sex are more easily combined in a quasi-permanent relation than in the scramble and excitement of parties and alcoholic stimulation. There is no reason under the sun why it should be more expensive for two young people to live together than to live separately, and therefore the economic reasons which at present lead to postponement of marriage would no longer operate. I have not the faintest doubt that

Judge Lindsey's plan, if embodied in the law, would have a very beneficent influence, and that this influence would be such as all might agree to be a gain from a moral point of view.

Nevertheless, Judge Lindsey's proposals were received with a howl of horror by all middle-aged persons and all newspapers throughout the length and breadth of America. It was said that he was attacking the sanctity of the home; it was said that in tolerating marriages not intended to lead at once to children he was opening the floodgates to legalised lust; it was said that he enormously exaggerated the prevalence of extra-marital sexual relations, that he was slandering pure American womanhood, and that most business men remained cheerfully continent up to the age of thirty or thirty-five. All these things were said, and I try to think that among those who said them were some who believed them. I listened to many invectives against Judge Lindsey, but I came away with the impression that the arguments which were regarded as decisive were two. First, that Judge Lindsey's proposals would not have been approved by Christ; and second, that they were not approved by even the more liberal of American divines. The second of these arguments appeared to be considered the more weighty, and indeed rightly, since the other is purely hypothetical, and incapable of being substantiated. I never heard any person advance any argument even pretending to show that Judge Lindsey's proposals would diminish human happiness. This consideration, indeed, I was forced to conclude, is thought wholly unimportant by those who uphold traditional morality.

For my part, while I am quite convinced that companionate marriage would be a step in the right direction, and would do a great deal of good, I do not think that it goes far enough. I think that all sex relations which do not involve children should be regarded as a purely private affair, and that if a man and a woman choose to live together without having children, that should be no one's business but their own. I should not hold it desirable that either a man or a woman should enter upon the serious business of a marriage intended to lead to children without having had previous sexual experience. There is a great mass of evidence to show that the first experience of sex should be with a person who has previous knowledge. The sexual act in human beings is not instinctive, and apparently never has been since it ceased to be performed *a tergo*. And apart from this argument, it seems absurd to ask people to enter upon a relation intended to be lifelong, without any previous knowledge as to their sexual compatibility. It is just as absurd as it would be if a man intending to buy a house were not allowed to view it until he had completed the purchase. The proper course, if the biological function of marriage were adequately recognised, would be to say that no marriage should be legally binding until the wife's first pregnancy. At present a marriage is null if sexual intercourse is impossible, but children, rather than sexual intercourse, are the true purpose of marriage, which should therefore be not regarded as consummated until such time as there is a prospect of children. This view depends, at least in part, upon that separation between procreation and mere sex which has been brought about by contraceptives. Contraceptives have altered the whole aspect of sex and marriage, and have made distinctions necessary which could formerly have been ignored. People may come together for sex alone, as occurs in prostitution, or for companionship involving a sexual element, as in Judge Lindsey's companionate marriage, or, finally, for the purpose of rearing a family. These are all different, and no morality can be adequate to modern circumstances which confounds them in one indiscriminate total.

Chapter 13

The Family at the Present Day

The reader may by this time have forgotten that in Chapters 2 and 3 we considered matrilineal and patriarchal families, and their bearing upon primitive views of sexual ethics. It is now time to resume the consideration of the family, which affords the only rational basis for limitations of sexual freedom. We have come to the end of a long parenthesis on Sex and Sin, a connection not invented by the early Christians, but exploited by them to the uttermost, and embodied now in the spontaneous moral judgments of most of us. I shall not trouble further with the theological view that in sex as such there is something wicked which can only be eliminated by the combination of marriage with the desire for offspring. The subject we have now to consider is the degree of stability in sex relations demanded by the interests of children. That is to say, we have to consider the family as a reason for stable marriage. This question is far from simple. It is clear that the gain which a child derives from being a member of a family depends upon what the alternative is: there might be institutions for foundlings so admirable that they would be preferable to the great majority of families. We have also to consider whether any essential part in family life is played by the father, since it is only on his account that feminine virtue has been thought essential to the family. We have to examine the effect of the family upon the individual psychology of the child – a subject dealt with in a somewhat sinister spirit by Freud. We have to consider the effect of economic systems in increasing or diminishing the importance of the father. We have to ask ourselves whether we should wish to see the State taking the place of the father, or possibly even, as Plato suggested, of both father and mother. And even supposing that we decide in favour of both father and mother as affording the best environment for the child in normal cases, we still have to consider the very numerous instances in which one or other is unfit for the responsibility of parenthood, or the two are so incompatible that separation is desirable in the interests of the child.

Among those who are opposed to sexual freedom on theological grounds, it is customary to argue against divorce as being contrary to the interests of the children. This argument, however, when used by the theologically minded, is not a genuine one, as may be seen from the fact that such persons will not tolerate either divorce or contraceptives, even when one parent is syphilitic and the children are likely to be so also. Cases of this sort show that the appeal with a sob in the voice to the interests of little children, when pushed to an extreme, is only an excuse for cruelty. The whole question of the connection of marriage with the interests of children needs to be considered without prejudice, and with the realisation that the answer is not obvious from the start. At this point, a few words of recapitulation are desirable.

The family is a pre-human institution, whose biological justification is that the help of the father during pregnancy and lactation tends to the survival of the young. But as we saw in the case of the Trobriand Islanders, and as we may safely infer in the case of the anthropoid apes, this help, under primitive conditions, is not given for quite the same reasons which actuate a father in a civilised community. The primitive father does not know that the child has any biological connection with himself; the child is the offspring of the female whom he loves. This fact he knows, since he has seen the child born, and it is this fact that produces the instinctive tie between him and the child. At this stage he sees no biological importance in safeguarding his wife's virtue, although no doubt he will feel instinctive jealousy if her infidelity is thrust upon his notice. At this stage, also, he has no sense of property in the child. The child is the property of his wife and his wife's brother, but his own relation with the child is merely one of affection.

With the development of intelligence, however, man is bound sooner or later to eat of the tree of the knowledge of good and evil. He becomes aware that the child springs from his seed, and he must therefore make sure of his wife's virtue. The wife and the child become his property, and at a certain level of economic development they may be very valuable property. He brings religion to bear, to cause his wife and children to have a sense of duty towards him. With children this is especially important, for although he is stronger than they are when they are young, the time will come when he will be decrepit while they will be in the vigour of manhood. At this stage, it is vitally necessary to his happiness that they should reverence him. The Commandment on this subject is deceitfully phrased. It should run: 'Honour thy father and thy mother that *their* days may be long in the land.' The horror of parricide which one finds in early civilisation shows how great was the temptation to be overcome; for a crime which we cannot imagine ourselves committing, such as cannibalism for example, fails to inspire us with any genuine horror.

It was the economic conditions of early pastoral and agricultural communities that brought the family to its fullest fruition. Slave labour was, for most people, unavailable, and therefore the easiest way to acquire labourers was to breed them. In order to make sure that they should work for their father, it was necessary that the institution of the family should be sanctified by the whole weight of religion and morals. Gradually primogeniture extended family unity to collateral branches, and enhanced the power of the head of the family. Kingship and aristocracy depend essentially upon this order of ideas, and even divinity, since Zeus was the father of gods and men.

Up to this point, the growth of civilisation had increased the strength of the family. From this point onward, however, an opposite movement has taken place, until the family in the Western world has become a mere shadow of what it was. The causes which brought about the decay of the family were partly economic and partly cultural. In its fullest development, it was never very suitable either to urban populations or to seafaring people. Commerce has been in all ages except ours the chief cause of culture, since it has brought men into relations with customs other than their own, and has thus emancipated them from tribal prejudice. Accordingly we find, among seafaring Greeks, much less slavery to the family than among their contemporaries. Other examples of the emancipating influence of the sea are to be found in Venice, in Holland, and in Elizabethan England. This, however, is beside the point. The only point which concerns us is that when one member of a family went on a long voyage while the rest stayed at home, he was inevitably emancipated from family control, and the family was proportionately weakened. The influx of rural populations into the towns, which is characteristic of all periods of rising civilisation, had the same kind of effect as marine commerce in weakening the family. Another influence, perhaps even more important where the lower strata of society were concerned, was slavery. The master had little respect for the family relations of his slaves. He could part husbands and wives whenever he felt so disposed, and he could, of course, himself have intercourse with any female slave who pleased him. These influences, it is true, did not weaken the aristocratic family, which was kept coherent by the desire for prestige, and for success in the Montague-and-Capulet brawls which characterised ancient city life as much as the city life of Italy in the latter Middle Ages and the Renaissance. Aristocracy, however, lost its importance during the first century of the Roman Empire, and Christianity, which ultimately conquered, had been at first a religion of slaves and proletarians. The previous weakening of the family in those social classes no doubt accounts for the fact that early Christianity was somewhat hostile to it, and formulated an ethic in which the place of the family was much less than in any previous ethic, except that of Buddhism. In the ethic of Christianity, it is the relation of the soul to God that is important, not the relation of man to his fellow-men.

The case of Buddhism, however, should warn us against an undue emphasis upon the purely economic causation of religions. I do not know enough of the condition of India at the time when Buddhism spread to be able to assign economic causes for its emphasis upon the individual soul, and I am rather doubtful whether such causes existed. Throughout the time when Buddhism flourished in India, it appears to have been primarily a religion for princes, and it might have been expected that ideas connected with the family would have had a stronger hold upon them than upon any other class. Nevertheless, contempt of this world and the search for salvation became common, with the result that in Buddhist ethics the family holds a very subordinate place. Great religious leaders, with the exception of Mohammed – and Confucius, if he can be called religious – have in general been very indifferent to social and political considerations, and have sought rather to perfect the soul by meditation, discipline, and self-denial. The religions which have arisen in historical times, as opposed to those which one finds already in existence when historical records begin, have been, on the whole, individualistic, and have tended to suppose that a man could do his whole duty in solitude. They have, of course, insisted that if a man has social relations he must perform such recognised duties as belong to those relations, but they have not, as a rule, regarded the formation of those relations as in itself a duty. This is especially true of Christianity, which has always had an ambivalent attitude towards the family. 'Whoso loveth father or mother more than me is not worthy of me', we read in the Gospels, and this means, in effect, that a man should do what he thinks right, even if his parents think it wrong – a view to which an ancient Roman or an old-fashioned Chinese would not subscribe. This leaven of individualism in Christianity has worked slowly, but has tended gradually to weaken all social relations, especially among those who were most in earnest. This effect is less seen in Catholicism than in Protestantism, for in Protestantism the anarchic element contained in the principle that we ought to obey God rather than man came to the fore. To obey God means, in practice, to obey one's conscience, and men's consciences may differ. There must, therefore, be occasional conflicts between conscience and law, in which the true Christian will feel bound to honour the man who follows his own conscience rather than the dictates of the law.[1] In early civilisation, the father was God; in Christianity, God is the Father, with the result that the authority of the merely human parent is weakened.

The decay of the family in quite recent times is undoubtedly to be attributed in the main to the industrial revolution, but it had already begun before that event, and its beginnings were inspired by individualistic theory. Young people asserted the right to marry according to their own wishes, not according to the commands of their parents. The habit of married sons living in their father's house died out. It became customary for sons to leave home to earn their living as soon as their education was ended. So long as small children could work in factories, they remained a source of livelihood to their parents until they died of overwork; but the Factory Acts put an end to this form of exploitation, in spite of the protests of those

---

[1] As an example of this, we may note the leniency of Lord Hugh Cecil to conscientious objectors during the war.

who lived on it. From being a means of livelihood, children came to be a financial burden. At this stage, contraceptives became known, and the fall in the birth-rate began. There is much to be said for the view that the average man in all ages has had as many children as it paid him to have, no more and no less. At any rate this seems to be true of Australian aborigines, Lancashire cotton operatives, and British peers. I do not pretend that this view can be maintained with theoretical exactness, but it is not so far from the truth as one might be inclined to suppose.

The position of the family in modern times has been weakened even in its last stronghold by the action of the State. In its great days, the family consisted of an elderly patriarch, a large number of grown-up sons, their wives and their children – perhaps their children's children – all living together in one house, all co-operating as one economic unit, all combined against the outer world as strictly as the citizens of a militaristic modern nation. Nowadays the family is reduced to the father and mother and their younger children, by the decree of the State, spend most of their time at school, and learn there what the State thinks good for them, not what their parents desire. (To this, however, religion is a partial exception.) So far from having power of life and death over his children, as the Roman father had, the British father is liable to be prosecuted for cruelty if he treats his child as most fathers a hundred years ago would have thought essential for a moral upbringing. The State provides medical and dental care, and feeds the child if the parents are destitute. The functions of the father are thus reduced to a minimum, since most of them have been taken over by the State. With advancing civilisation, this is inevitable. In a primitive state of affairs, the father was necessary, as he is among birds and anthropoid apes, for economic reasons, and also to protect the young and their mother from violence. The latter function was long ago taken over by the State. A child whose father is dead is no more likely to be murdered than one whose father is living. The economic function of the father can be performed, in the well-to-do classes, more efficiently if he is dead than if he is living, since he can leave his money to his children, without having to use up part of it on his own maintenance. Among those who depend upon earned money, the father is still economically useful, but so far as wage-earners are concerned this utility is being continually diminished by the humanitarian sentiment of the community, which insists that the child should receive a certain minimum of care, even if he has no father to pay for it. It is in the middle classes that the father is at present of most importance, for so long as he lives and earns a good income, he can give his children those advantages in the way of an expensive education which will enable them in their turn to preserve their social and economic status, whereas if he dies while the children are still young, there is a considerable chance that they may sink in the social scale. The precariousness of this state of affairs is, however, much diminished by the custom of life insurance, by means of which, even in the professional classes, a prudent father can do much to diminish his own utility.

In the modern world, the great majority of fathers are too hardworked to see much of their own children. In the morning they are too busy getting off to work to have time for conversation; in the evening, when they get home, the children are (or ought to be) in bed. One hears stories of children who only know of their father as 'that man who comes for the weekend'. In the serious business of caring for the child, fathers can seldom participate; in fact this duty is shared between mothers and education authorities. It is true that the father often has a strong affection for his children in spite of the small amount of time that he can spend with them. On any Sunday, in any of the poorer quarters of London, large numbers of fathers may be seen with their young children, evidently rejoicing in the brief opportunity of getting to know them. But whatever may be the case from the father's point of view, from that of the child this is a play relation, without serious importance.

In the upper and professional classes, the custom is to leave children to nurses while they are young, and then send them to a boarding-school. The mother chooses the nurse, and the father chooses the school, so that they preserve intact their sense of power over their offspring, which working-class parents are not allowed to do. But so far as intimate contact is concerned, there is less, as a rule, between mother and child among the well-to-do than among wage-earners. The father has a play relation with his children in holidays, but has no more part in their real education than a working class father. He has, of course, economic responsibility and the power of deciding where they shall be educated, but his personal contact with them is not usually of a very serious kind.

When a child reaches adolescence, there is very apt to be a conflict between parents and child, since the latter considers himself to be by now quite capable of managing his own affairs, while the former are filled with parental solicitude, which is often a disguise for love of power. Parents consider, usually, that the various moral problems which arise in adolescence are peculiarly their province. The opinions they express, however, are so dogmatic that the young seldom confide in them, and usually go their own way in secret. It cannot be said, therefore, that at this stage most parents are much use.

So far we have been considering only the weakness of the modern family. We must now consider in what respects it is still strong.

The family is important at the present day, more through the emotions with which it provides parents than for any other reason. Parental emotions in men as well as in women are perhaps more important than any others in their power of influencing action. Both men and women who have children as a rule regulate their lives largely with reference to them, and children cause perfectly ordinary men and women to act unselfishly in certain ways, of which perhaps life insurance is the most definite and measurable. The economic man of a hundred years ago was never provided in the textbooks with children, though undoubtedly he had them in the imagination of the economists, who, however, took it for granted that the general competition which they postulated did not exist between fathers and sons. Clearly, the psychology of life insurance lies wholly outside the cycle of motives dealt with in the classical political economy. Yet that political economy was not psychologically autonomous, since the desire for property is very intimately bound up with parental feelings. Rivers went so far as to suggest that all private property is derivative from family feelings. He mentions certain birds which have private property in land during the breeding season, but at no other time. I think most men can testify that they become far more acquisitive when they have children than they were before. This effect is one which is, in the popular sense, instinctive, that is to say, it is spontaneous, and springs from subconscious sources. I think that in this respect the family has been of incalculable importance to the economic development of mankind, and is still a dominating factor among those who are sufficiently prosperous to have a, chance to save money.

There is apt to be on this point a curious misunderstanding between fathers and children. A man who works hard in business will tell his idle son that he has slaved all his life solely for the benefit of his children. The son, on the contrary, would much rather have a fiver and a little kindness now than a fortune when his father dies. The son notices, moreover, quite correctly, that his father goes to the City from force of habit and not the least from parental affection. The son is therefore as sure that his father is a humbug as the father is that his son is a wastrel. The son, however, is unjust.

He sees his father in middle age, when all his habits are formed, and he does not realise the obscure, unconscious forces which led to the formation of those habits. The father, perhaps, may have suffered from poverty in his youth, and when his first child was born his instinct may have made him swear that no child of his should endure what he had had to suffer. Such a resolution is important and vital, and therefore need never be repeated in consciousness, since without the need of repetition it dominates conduct ever after. This is one way in which the family is still a very powerful force.

From the point of view of the young child, the important thing about parents is that from them the child gets an affection not given to anyone else except his brothers and sisters. This is partly good and partly bad. I propose to consider the psychological effects of the family upon children in the next chapter. I shall therefore say no more about it at the present moment than that it is clearly a very important element in character formation, and that children brought up away from parents may be expected to differ considerably, whether for better or for worse, from normal children.

In an aristocratic society, or indeed in any society permitting of personal eminence, the family is, in regard to certain important individuals, a mark connected with historical continuity. Observation seems to show that people whose name is Darwin do better work in science than they would do if their name had been changed to Snooks in infancy. I conceive that if surnames descended through the female instead of the male, effects of this kind would be exactly as strong as they are now. It is quite impossible to apportion the shares of heredity and environment respectively in such cases, but I am quite convinced that family tradition plays a very considerable part in the phenomena which Galton and his disciples attribute to heredity. One might give as an example of the influence of family tradition the reason said to have caused Samuel Butler to invent his doctrine of unconscious memory and to advocate a neo-Lamarckian theory of heredity. The reason was that for family reasons he felt it necessary to disagree with Charles Darwin. His grandfather (it seems) quarrelled with Darwin's grandfather, his father with his father, so he must quarrel with him. Thus Shaw's Methuselah is what it is, owing to the fact that Darwin and Butler had ill-tempered grandfathers.

Perhaps the greatest importance of the family, in these days of contraceptives, is that it preserves the habit of having children. If a man were going to have no property in his child, and no opportunity of affectionate relations with it, he would see little point in begetting it. It would, of course, with a slight change in our economic institutions, be possible to have families consisting of mothers only, but it is not such families that I am considering at the present time, since they afford no motives for sexual virtue, and it is the family as a reason for stable marriage that concerns us in the present work. It may be – and indeed I think it far from improbable – that the father will be completely eliminated before long, except among the rich (supposing the rich to be not abolished by Socialism). In that case, women will share their children with the State, not with an individual father. They will have such number of children as they desire, and the fathers will have no responsibility. Indeed, if the mothers are at all of a promiscuous disposition, fatherhood may be impossible to determine. But if this comes about, it will make a profound change in the psychology and activities of men, far more profound, I believe, than most people would suppose. Whether the effect upon men would be good or bad, I do not venture to say. It would eliminate from their lives the only emotion equal in importance to sex love. It would make sex love itself more trivial. It would make it far more difficult to take an interest in anything after one's own death. It would make men less active and probably cause them to retire earlier from work. It would diminish their interest in history and their sense of the continuity of historical tradition. At the same time it would eliminate the most fierce and savage passion to which civilised men are liable, namely the fury which is felt in defending wives and children from attacks by coloured populations. I think it would make men less prone to war, and probably less acquisitive. To strike a balance between good and bad effects is scarcely possible, but it is evident that the effects would be profound and far-reaching. The patriarchal family, therefore, is still important, although it is doubtful how long it will remain so.

Chapter 14

The Family in Individual Psychology

I wish to consider in this chapter how the character of the individual is affected by family relations. This subject is threefold: there is the effect upon children, the effect upon the mother, and the effect upon the father. It is, of course, undoubtedly difficult to disentangle these three, since the family is a closely-knit unit, and anything that affects the parents affects also their influence upon the children. Nevertheless, I shall attempt to divide the discussion into these three heads, and it is natural to begin with the children, since everybody is a child in the family before being a parent.

If we are to believe Freud, the emotions of a young child towards the other members of his family have a somewhat desperate character. A boy hates his father, whom he regards as a sexual rival. He feels, in regard to his mother, emotions which are viewed with the utmost abhorrence by traditional morality. He hates his brothers and sisters because they absorb some part of the parental attention, of which he would like the whole to be concentrated upon himself. In later life, the effects of these turbulent passions are of the most diverse and terrible kinds, varying from homosexuality at best to mania at worst.

This Freudian doctrine has caused less horror than one might have expected. It is true that professors have been dismissed from their posts for believing it, and that the British police deported one of the best men of his generation[1]

[1] Homer Lane.

for acting upon it. But such is the influence of Christian asceticism that people have been more shocked by Freud's insistence upon sex than by his picture of infantile hatreds. We, however, must try to make up our minds without prejudice as to the truth or falsehood of Freud's opinions concerning the passions of children. I will confess, to begin with, that a considerable experience of young children during recent years has led me to the view that there is much more truth in Freud's theories than I had formerly supposed. Nevertheless, I still think that they represent only one side of the truth, and a side which can easily, with a little good sense on the part of parents, be rendered very unimportant.

Let us begin with the Oedipus complex. Infantile sexuality is undoubtedly stronger than anybody thought before Freud. I think, even, that heterosexuality is stronger in early childhood than one would gather from Freud's writings. It is not difficult for an unwise mother quite unintentionally to centre the heterosexual feelings of a young son upon herself, and it is true that, if this is done, the evil consequences pointed out by Freud will probably ensue. This is, however, much less likely to occur if the mother's sexual life is satisfying to her, for in that case she will not look to her child for a type of emotional satisfaction which ought to be sought only from adults. The parental impulse in its purity is an impulse to care for the young, not to demand affection from them, and if a woman is happy in her sexual life she will abstain spontaneously from all improper demands for emotional response from her child. For this reason a happy woman is likely to be a better mother than an unhappy one. No woman, however, can make sure of being always happy, and at times of unhappiness a certain amount of self-control may be necessary to avoid demanding too much of children. This degree of self-control is not very difficult to practice, but in former times the need for it was not realised, and a mother was thought to be behaving quite properly in lavishing continual caresses upon her children.

The heterosexual emotions of young children can find a natural, wholesome and innocent outlet with other children; in this form they are a part of play, and, like all play, they afford a preparation for adult activities. After the age of three or four, a child needs, for his or her emotional development, the company of other children of both sexes, not only brothers and sisters, who are necessarily older or younger, but contemporaries. The modern small family, unadulterated, is too stuffy and confined for healthy development during the early years, but that does not mean that it is undesirable as an ingredient in the childish environment.

It is not only mothers who are liable to arouse in the young child undesirable kinds of affection. Servant-girls and nurses, and, in later years, schoolteachers, are quite as dangerous, indeed even more so, since they are, as a rule, sexually starved. Education authorities are of opinion that those who have to deal with the young ought always to be unhappy spinsters. This view shows gross psychological ignorance, and could not be entertained by anyone who had watched closely the emotional development of young children.

Jealousy of brothers and sisters is very common in families, and is sometimes a cause, in later life, of homicidal mania as well as of less serious nervous disorders. Except in mild forms, it is not at all difficult to prevent, provided parents and others who have charge of the young take a little trouble to control their own behaviour. There must, of course, be no favouritism – the most meticulous justice must be observed in regard to toys and treats and attention. At the birth of a new brother or sister, pains must be taken to prevent the others from imagining that they have become less important to their parents than they were. Wherever serious cases of jealousy occur, it will be found, I think that these simple precepts have been disregarded.

We arrive, therefore, at certain conditions which must be fulfilled if the psychological effect of family life upon children is to be good. The parents, and especially the mother, must if possible not be unhappy in their sexual life. Both parents must avoid that kind of emotional relation with their children that calls for a response not suitable in infancy. There must be no kind of preference as between brothers and sisters, but all must be treated with a'completely impartial justice. And after the age of three or four, the home should not be the sole environment of the child, but a considerable part of its day should be spent in the society of contemporaries. Given these conditions, the bad effects feared by Freud are, I think, very unlikely to occur.

On the other hand, parental affection, when it is of the right sort, undoubtedly furthers a child's development. Children whose mothers do not feel a warm affection for them are apt to be thin and nervous, and sometimes they develop such faults as kleptomania. The affection of parents makes infants feel safe in this dangerous world, and gives them boldness in experimentation and in exploration of their environment. It is necessary to a child's mental life to feel himself the object of warm affection, for he is instinctively aware of his help-lessness, and of his need of a protection which only affection can ensure. If a child is to grow up happy, expansive, and fearless, he needs a certain warmth in his environment which is difficult to get except through parental affection.

There is another service which a wise father and mother can perform for their children, although until quite recent times they hardly ever did so. This is, that they can introduce them to the facts of sex and parenthood in the best possible way. If children learn of sex as a relation between their parents to which they owe their own existence, they learn of it in its best form and in connection with its biological purpose. In old days, they practically always learned of it first as the subject of ribald jokes and as a source of pleasures considered disgraceful. This first initiation, by means of secret indecent talk, usually made an indelible impression, so that it was ever after impossible to have a decent attitude on any subject connected with sex.

To decide whether family life is on the whole desirable or undesirable, we must, of course, consider what are the only practical alternatives. They seem to be two: first, the matriarchal family, and second, public institutions such as orphan asylums. To cause either of these to become the rule would require considerable economic changes. We may suppose them carried out, and consider the effect upon the pschology of children.

To begin with the matriarchal family. Here one supposes that the children will know only one parent, that a woman will have a child when she feels that she wants one, but without expecting the father to take any particular interest in it, and not necessarily choosing the same father for different children. Assuming the economic arrangements to be satisfactory, would children suffer much by such a system? What, in effect, is the psychological use of a father to his children? I think perhaps the most important use lies in the last point mentioned, namely the connecting of sex with married love and procreation. There is also, after the first years of infancy, a very definite gain in being brought into contact with a masculine as well as a feminine outlook on life. To boys especially, this is intellectually important. At the same time, I cannot see that the gain is very profound. Children whose fathers have died while they were infants do not, so far as I know, turn out on the average any worse than other children. No doubt the ideal father is better than none, but many fathers are so far from ideal that their non-existence might be a positive advantage to children.

What has just been said depends upon the supposition of a convention quite different from that obtaining at present. Where a convention exists, children suffer through its being infringed, since there is hardly anything so painful to a child as the feeling of being in any way odd. This consideration

applies to divorce in our present society. A child who has been
used to two parents and has become attached to them both
finds a divorce between them destructive of his whole sense of
security. Indeed, he is likely in these circumstances to develop phobias and other nervous disorders. When once a child
has become attached to both his parents, they take a very
grave responsibility if they separate. I think, therefore, that a
society in which fathers have no place would be better for
children than one in which divorce is frequent though still
regarded as exceptional.

I do not see much to be said for Plato's proposal to separate
children from their mothers as well as from their fathers. For
the reasons already mentioned, I think that parental affection
is essential to a child's development, and that while it might
suffice to receive this affection only from one parent, it would
certainly be very regrettable if it were not received from
either. From the point of view of sexual morals, which is that
with which we are primarily concerned, the important question is the utility of the father. As to this, while it is very
difficult to say anything positively, the conclusion seems to be
that in fortunate cases he has a certain limited usefulness,
while in unfortunate cases he may easily, by tyranny and ill-
temper and a quarrelsome disposition do far more harm than
good. The case for fathers, from the point of view of children's psychology, is not therefore a very strong one.

The importance of the family, as it exists at present, in the
psychology of mothers is very difficult to estimate. I think that
during pregnancy and lactation a woman has, as a rule, a
certain instinctive tendency to desire a man's protection – a
feeling, no doubt, inherited from the anthropoid apes. Probably a woman who, in our present rather harsh world, has to
dispense with this protection tends to become somewhat unduly combative and self-assertive. These feelings, however,
are only in part instinctive. They would be greatly weakened,
and in some cases wholly abolished, if the State gave adequate

care to expectant and nursing mothers and to young children. I think perhaps the chief harm that would be done to women by abolition of the father's place in the home would be the diminution in the intimacy and seriousness of their relations with the male sex. Human beings are so constructed that each sex has much to learn from the other, but mere sex relations, even when they are passionate, do not suffice for these lessons. Co-operation in the serious business of rearing children, and companionship through the long years involved, bring about a relation more important and more enriching to both parties than any that would exist if men had no responsibility for their children. And I do not think that mothers who live in a purely feminine atmosphere, or whose contacts with men are trivial, will, except in a minority of cases, be quite so good for their children from the point of view of emotional education as those who are happily married and co-operating at each stage with their husbands. One must, however, in a great many cases set other considerations over against these. If a woman is actively unhappy in her marriage – and this, after all is by no means an uncommon occurrence – her unhappiness makes it very difficult for her to have the right kind of emotional poise in dealing with her children. In such cases she could undoubtedly be a better mother if she were quit of the father. We are thus led to the entirely trivial conclusion that happy marriages are good, while unhappy ones are bad.

Much the most important question in relation to the family in individual psychology is the effect upon the father. We have already repeatedly had occasion to point out the significance of paternity and its attendant passions. We have seen what part it played in early history in connection with the growth of the patriarchal family and the subjection of women, and we can judge from this what a powerful passion paternal feeling must be. For reasons not easy to fathom, it is not nearly so strong in highly civilised communities as it is elsewhere. Upper-class Romans in the time of the Empire apparently ceased to feel it, and many intellectualised men in our own day are nearly or quite destitute of it. Nevertheless, it is still felt by the great majority of men, even in the most civilised communities. It is for this reason, rather than for the sake of sex, that men marry, for it is not difficult to obtain sexual satisfaction without marriage. There is a theory that the desire for children is commoner among women than among men, but my own impression, for what it is worth, is exactly the contrary. In a very large number of modern marriages, the children are a concession on the part of the woman to the man's desires. A woman, after all, has to face labour and pain and possible loss of beauty in order to bring a child into the world, whereas a man has no such grounds for anxiety. A man's reasons for wishing to limit his family are generally economic; these reasons operate equally with the woman, but she has her own special reasons as well. The strength of the desire that men feel for children is evident when one considers the loss of material comfort that professional men deliberately incur when they undertake to educate a family in the expensive manner that their class considers necessary.

Would men beget children if they were not going to enjoy the rights which paternity confers at present? Some people would say that if they were not going to have responsibilities they would beget them recklessly. I do not believe this. A man who desires a child desires the responsibilities which it entails. And in these days of contraceptives a man will not often have a child as a mere incident in his pursuit of pleasure. Of course, whatever the state of the law might be, it would always be open to a man and woman to live in a permanent union in which the man could enjoy something of what now comes through fatherhood; but if law and custom were adapted to the view that children belong to the mother alone, women would feel that anything approximating to marriage as we know it now was an infraction of the independence, and involved a needless loss of that complete ownership over their children which they would otherwise enjoy. We must therefore expect that men would not often succeed in persuading women to concede rights legally guaranteed to them.

Something was said in the last chapter as to the effect of such a system upon male psychology. It would, I believe, immensely diminish the seriousness of men's relations to women, making them more and more a matter of mere pleasure, not an intimate union of heart and mind and body. It would tend towards a certain triviality in all personal relations, so that a man's serious emotions would be concerned with his career, his country, or some quite impersonal subject. All this, however, is expressed somewhat too generally, for men differ profoundly one from another, and what to one might be a grave deprivation might to another be entirely satisfactory. My belief is, though I put it forward with some hesitation, that the elimination of paternity as a recognized social relation would tend to make men's emotional life trivial and thin, causing in the end a slowly growing boredom and despair, in which procreation would gradually die out, leaving the human race to be replenished by stocks that had preserved the older convention. The boredom and triviality would, I think, be unavoidable. The diminution of population could, of course, be guarded against by paying women a sufficient sum for taking up the profession of motherhood. This will presumably be done before long, if militarism remains as strong as it is at present. But this line of thought belongs with the consideration of the population question, which will be dealt with in a later chapter. I shall not, therefore, at present pursue it farther.

Chapter 15

The Family and the State

The family, though it has a biological origin, is in civilised communities a product of legal enactment. Marriage is regulated by law, and the rights of parents over their children are minutely determined. Where there is no marriage, the father has no rights, and the child belongs exclusively to the mother. But although the law means to uphold the family, it has in modern times increasingly intervened between parents and children, and is gradually becoming, against the wish and intention of law-makers, one of the chief engines for the break-up of the family system. This has happened through the fact that bad parents cannot be relied upon to take as much care of their children as the general feeling of the community considers necessary. And not only bad parents, but such as are very poor, require the intervention of the State to secure their children from disaster. In the early nineteenth century, the proposal to interfere with the labour of children in factories was fiercely resisted on the ground that it would weaken parental responsibility. Although the English law did not, like that of ancient Rome, allow parents to kill their children quickly and painlessly, it did permit them to drain their children of life by a slow agony of toil. This sacred right was defended by parents, employers, and economists. Nevertheless, the moral sense of the community was revolted by such abstract pedantry, and the Factory Acts were passed. The next step was a more important one, namely the inauguration of compulsory education. This is a really serious interference with the rights of parents. For a large number of hours on all days except holidays, the children have to be away from home, learning things that the State considers necessary for them to know and what the parents think about the matter is legally irrelevant. Through the schools, the control of the State over the lives of children is being gradually extended. Their health is cared for, even if their parents are Christian Scientists. If they are mentally deficient, they are sent to special schools. If they are necessitous, they may be fed. Boots may be supplied if the parents cannot afford them. If the children arrive at school showing signs of parental ill-treatment, the parents are likely to suffer penal consequences. In old days, parents had a right to the earnings of their children as long as their children were under age; now, although it may be difficult in practice for children to withhold their earnings, they have the right to do so, and this right can be enforced when circumstances arise which make it important. One of the few rights remaining to parents in the wage-earning class is that of having their children taught any brand of superstition that may be shared by a large number of parents in the same neighbourhood. And even this right has been taken away from parents in many countries.

To this process of substituting the State for the father no clear limit can be set. It is the functions of the father rather than of the mother that the State has taken over, since it performs for the child such services as the father would otherwise have to pay for. In the upper and middle classes this process has hardly taken place at all, and consequently the father remains more important, and the family more stable, among the well-to-do than among the wage-earners. Where Socialism is taken seriously, as in Soviet Russia, the abolition or complete transformation of educational institutions previously intended for the children of the rich is recognised as an important and vitally necessary undertaking. It is difficult to imagine this taking place in England. I have seen prominent English Socialists foam at the mouth at the suggestion that all children ought to go to elementary schools. 'What? My children associate with the children of the slums? Never!' they exclaim. Oddly enough, they fail to realise how profoundly the division between the classes is bound up with the educational system.

The present tendency in all countries is towards a continually increasing interference of the State with the power and functions of the father in the wage-earning class, without any corresponding interference (except in Russia) in other classes. The effect of this is to produce two rather different kinds of outlook among the rich and the poor respectively, with a weakening of the family where the poor are concerned, and no corresponding change as regards the rich. It may, I think, be assumed that humanitarian sentiment towards children, which has caused past interventions of the State, will continue, and will cause more and more interventions. The fact that an immense percentage of children in the poor parts of London, and still more in the industrial cities of the North, suffer from rickets, for example, is one which calls for public action. The parents cannot deal with the evil, however much they may wish to do so, since it requires conditions of diet and fresh air and light which they are not in a position to provide. It is wasteful as well as cruel to allow children to be physically ruined during the first year of their lives, and as hygiene and diet come to be better understood, there will be an increasing demand that children should not be made to suffer unnecessary damage. It is true, of course, that there is a vehement political resistance to all such suggestions. The well-to-do in every London borough band themselves together to keep down the rates, that is to say, to ensure that as little as possible shall be done to alleviate illness and misery among the poor. When local authorities, as in Poplar, take really effective measures to diminish infant morality, they are put in prison.[1] Nevertheless, this resistance of the rich is continually being overcome, and the health of the poor is continually being improved. We may therefore confidently expect that the functions of the State in regard to the care of wage-earners' children will be extended rather than curtailed in the near future, with a corresponding diminution in the functions of fathers. The biological purpose of the father is to protect children during their years of helplessness, and when this biological function is taken over by the State, the father loses his *raison d'être*. We must therefore, in capitalistic communities expect an increasing division of society into two castes, the rich preserving the family in its old form, and the poor looking more and more to the State to perform the economic functions traditionally belonging to the father.

More radical transformations of the family have been envisaged in Soviet Russia, but in view of the fact that eighty per cent of the population consists of peasants, among whom the family is still as strong as it was in Western Europe in the Middle Ages, the theories of Communists are likely to affect only a comparatively small urban section. We may therefore get in Russia the exact antithesis to the situation we have been considering in capitalistic countries, namely an upper class which dispenses with the family and a lower class which retains it.

There is another powerful force which is working in the direction of the elimination of the father, and this is the desire of women for economic independence. The women who have been most politically vocal hitherto have been unmarried women, but this state of affairs is likely to be temporary. The wrongs of married women are at the moment much more

[1] In 1922 the infant death-rate was five per thousand lower in Poplar than in Kensington; in 1926, after the restoration of legality in Poplar had done its beneficent work, it was ten per thousand higher in Poplar than in Kensington.

serious than those of unmarried women. The teacher who
marries is treated in just the same way as the teacher who lives
in open sin. Even public maternity doctors, if they are
women, have to be unmarried. The motive for all this is not
that married women are supposed to be unfit for the work, nor
is it that there is any legal barrier to their employment; on the
contrary, a law was passed not many years ago explicitly
laying it down that no woman should suffer any disability
through marriage. The whole motive for the non-employment
of married women is a masculine desire to preserve economic
power over them. It is not to be supposed that women will
submit indefinitely to such tyranny. It is, of course, a little
difficult to find a party to take up their cause, since the Conservatives love the home, and the Labour Party loves the
working man. Nevertheless, now that women are a majority of
the electorate, it is not to be supposed that they will submit
for ever to being kept in the background. Their claims, if
recognised, are likely to have a profound effect upon the
family. There are two different ways in which married women
might acquire economic independence. One is that of remaining employed in the kind of work that they were engaged upon
before marriage. This involves giving their children over to
the care of others, and would lead to a very great extension of
crèches and nursery schools, the logical consequence of which
would be the elimination of the mother as well as of the father
from all importance in the child's psychology. The other
method would be that women with young children should
receive a wage from the State on condition of devoting themselves to the care of their children. This method would, of
course, be not alone adequate, and would need to be supplemented by provisions enabling women to return to ordinary work when their children ceased to be quite young. But
it would have the advantage of enabling women to care for their
children themselves without degrading dependence upon an
individual man. And it would recognise, what in these days is

more and more the case, that having a child, which was formerly a mere consequence of sexual gratification, is now a task
deliberately undertaken, which, since it redounds to the advantage of the State rather than of the parents, should be paid
for by the State, instead of entailing a grave burden upon the
father and mother. This last point is being recognised in the
advocacy of family allowances, but it is not yet recognised that
the payment for children should be made to the mother
alone. I think we may assume, however, that working-class
feminism will grow to the point where this is recognised, and
embodied in the law.

Assuming such a law to have been passed, its effects upon
family morals will depend upon how it has been drafted. The
law may be so drafted that a woman receives no payment if
her child is illegitimate; or again, it might be decreed that if
she can be proved even once guilty of adultery, the payment
should be made to her husband instead of to her. If such is the
law, it will become the duty of the local police to visit every
married woman and make an inquisition into her moral status.
The effect might be most elevating, but I doubt whether
those who were being elevated would altogether enjoy it. I
think there would presently come to be a demand that police
interference should cease, with the corollary that even the
mothers of illegitimate children should receive the allowance.
If that were done, the economic power of the father in the
wage-earning class would be completely at an end, and the
family would probably cease after a time to be bi-parental, the
father being of no more importance than among cats and dogs.

There is, however, in these days, on the part of the individual woman often such a horror of the home that I think
most women would very much prefer to be enabled to continue the work they were doing before marriage, rather than
to be paid for taking care of their own children. There would
be a sufficient number of women willing to leave their own
homes in order to look after young children in a crèche, be-

cause that would be professional work; but I do not think that most working women, if the choice were offered them, would be as happy being paid to look after their own children in the home as going out to work to earn wages at the job on which they were engaged before marriage. This, however, is purely a matter of opinion, and I cannot pretend that I have any conclusive grounds. However that may be, it seems, if there is any truth in what we have been saying, that the development of feminism among married women is likely, in the not distant future, even within the framework of capitalist society, to lead to the elimination of one if not both parents from the care of the young in the wage-earning class.

The revolt of women against the domination of men is a movement which, in its purely political sense, is practically completed, but in its wider aspects is still in its infancy. Gradually its remoter effects will work themselves out. The emotions which women are supposed to feel are still, as yet, a reflection of the interests and sentiments of men. You will read in the works of male novelists that women find physical pleasure in suckling their young; you can learn by asking any mother of your acquaintance that this is not the case, but until women had votes no man ever thought of doing so. Maternal emotions altogether have been so long slobbered over by men who saw in them subconsciously the means to their own domination that a considerable effort is required to arrive at what women sincerely feel in this respect. Until very recently, all decent women were supposed to desire children, but to hate sex. Even now, many men are shocked by women who frankly state that they do not desire children. Indeed, it is not uncommon for men to take it upon themselves to deliver homilies to such women. So long as women were in subjection, they did not dare to be honest about their own emotions, but professed those which were pleasing to the male. We cannot, therefore, argue from what has been hitherto supposed to be women's normal attitude towards children, for we may find that as women become fully emancipated their emotions turn out to be, in general, quite different from what has hitherto been thought. I think that civilisation, at any rate as it has hitherto existed, tends greatly to diminish women's maternal feelings. It is probable that a high civilisation will not in future be possible to maintain unless women are paid such sums for the production of children as to make them feel it worth while as a money-making career. If that were done it would, of course, be unnecessary that all women, or even a majority, should adopt this profession. It would be one profession among others, and would have to be undertaken with professional thoroughness. These, however, are speculations. The only point in them that seems fairly certain is that feminism in its later developments is likely to have a profound influence in breaking up the patriarchal family, which represents man's triumph over woman in prehistoric times.

The substitution of the State for the father, so far as it has yet gone in the West, is in the main a great advance. It has immensely improved the health of the community and the general level of education. It has diminished cruelty to children, and has made impossible such sufferings as those of David Copperfield. It may be expected to continue to raise the general level of physical health and intellectual attainment, especially by preventing the worst evils resulting from the family system where it goes wrong. There are, however, very grave dangers in the substitution of the State for the family. Parents, as a rule, are fond of their children, and do not regard them merely as material for political schemes. The State cannot be expected to have this attitude. The actual individuals who come in contact with children in institutions, for example school-teachers, may, if they are not too overworked and underpaid, retain something of the personal feeling that parents have. But teachers have little power; the power belongs to administrators. The administrators never see the children whose lives they control, and being of an administrative type (since otherwise they would not have obtained the posts they occupy), they are probably peculiarly apt to regard human beings, not as ends in themselves, but as material for some kind of construction. Moreover, the administrator invariably likes uniformity. It is convenient for statistics and pigeon-holing, and if it is the 'right' sort of uniformity it means the existence of a large number of human beings of the sort that he considers desirable. Children handed over to the mercy of institutions will therefore tend to be all alike, while the few who cannot conform to the recognised pattern will suffer persecution, not only from their fellows, but from the authorities. This means that many of those who have the greatest potentialities will be harried and tortured until their spirit is broken. It means that the vast majority, who succeed in conforming, will become very sure of themselves, very prone to persecution, and very incapable of listening patiently to any new idea. Above all, so long as the world remains divided into competing militaristic States, the substitution of public bodies for parents in education means an intensification of what is called patriotism, i.e. a willingness to indulge in mutual extermination without a moment's hesitation, whenever the Governments feel so inclined. Undoubtedly patriotism, so-called, is the gravest danger to which civilisation is at present exposed, and anything that increases its virulence is more to be dreaded than plague, pestilence, and famine. At present young people have a divided loyalty, on the one hand to their parents, on the other to the State. If it should happen that their sole loyalty was to the State, there is grave reason to fear that the world would become even more bloodthirsty than it is at present. I think, therefore, that so long as the problem of internationalism remains unsolved, the increasing share of the State in the education and care of children has dangers so grave as to outweigh its undoubted advantages.

If, on the other hand, an international Government were

established, capable of substituting law for force in disputes between nations, the situation would be entirely different. Such a Government could decree that nationalism in its more insane forms should be no part of the educational curriculum in any country. It could insist that loyalty to the international super-State should everywhere be taught, and that internationalism should be inculcated as a sentiment in place of the present devotion to the national flag. In that case, although the danger of too great uniformity and too severe a persecution of freaks would still exist, the danger of promoting war would be eliminated. Indeed, the control of the super-State over education would be a positive safeguard against war. The conclusion seems to be that the substitution of the State for the father would be a gain to civilisation if the State were international, but that so long as the State is national and militaristic it represents an increase of the risk to civilisation from war. The family is decaying fast, and internationalism is growing slowly. The situation, therefore, is one which justifies grave apprehensions. Nevertheless, it is not hopeless, since internationalism may grow more quickly in the future than it has done in the past. Fortunately, perhaps, we cannot foretell the future, and we have therefore the right to hope, if not to expect, that it may be an improvement upon the present.

Chapter 16

Divorce

Divorce as an institution has been permitted in most ages and countries for certain causes. It has never been intended to produce an alternative to the monogamic family, but merely to mitigate hardship where, for special reasons, the continuance of a marriage was felt to be intolerable. The law on the subject has been extraordinarily different in different ages and places, and varies at the present day, even within the United States, from the extreme of no divorce in South Carolina to the opposite extreme in Nevada.[1] In many non-Christian civilisations, divorce has been very easy for a husband to obtain, and in some it has also been easy for a wife. The Mosaic Law allows a husband to give a bill of divorcement; Chinese law allowed divorce provided the property which the wife had brought into the marriage was restored. The Catholic Church, on the ground that marriage is a sacrament, does not allow divorce for any purpose whatsoever, but in practice this severity is somewhat mitigated – especially where the great ones of the earth are concerned – by the fact that there are many grounds for nullity.[2] In Christian countries the

[1] In Nevada, the grounds are wilful desertion, conviction of felony or infamous crime, habitual gross drunkenness, impotency at the time of marriage continuing to the time of the divorce, extreme cruelty, neglect to provide for one year, insanity for two years. See *Sex in Civilization*, edited by V. F. Claverton and S. D. Schmalhausen. London: George Allen and Unwin Ltd, 1929, p. 224.

[2] It will be remembered that in the case of the Duke and Duchess of Marlborough it was held that the marriage was null because she had been forced into it, and this ground was considered valid in spite of the fact that they had lived together for years and had children.

leniency towards divorce has been proportional to the degree of Protestantism. Milton, as everyone knows, wrote in favour of it, because he was very Protestant. The English Church, in the days when it considered itself Protestant, recognised divorce for adultery, though for no other cause. Nowadays the great majority of clergymen in the Church of England are opposed to all divorce. Scandinavia has easy divorce laws. So have the most Protestant parts of America. Scotland is more favourable to divorce than England. In France, anti-clericalism produces easy divorce. In the Soviet Union divorce is permitted at the request of either party, but as neither social nor legal penalties attach to either adultery or illegitimacy in Russia, marriage has there lost the importance which it has elsewhere, at any rate so far as the governing classes are concerned.

One of the most curious things about divorce is the difference which has often existed between law and custom. The easiest divorce laws by no means always produce the greatest number of divorces. In China, before the recent upheavals, divorce was almost unknown, for in spite of the example of Confucius, it was not considered quite respectable. Sweden allows divorce by mutual consent, which is a ground not recognised in any State of America; yet I find that in 1922, the latest year for which I have comparable figures, the number of divorces per hundred thousand of the population was twenty-four in Sweden and 136 in the United States.[1] I think this distinction between law and custom is important, for while I favour a somewhat lenient law on the subject, there are to my mind, so long as the bi-parental family persists as the norm, strong reasons why custom should be against divorce, except in somewhat extreme cases. I take this view because I regard marriage not primarily as a sexual part-

[1] Since then the total number of divorces and nullities in Sweden increased from 1,531 in 1923 to 1,966 in 1927, while the rate per hundred marriages increased in USA from 13·4 to 15.

nership, but above all as an undertaking to co-operate in the procreation and rearing of children. It is possible, and even probable, as we have seen in earlier chapters, that marriage so understood may break down under the operation of various forces of which the economic are the chief, but if this should occur, divorce also would break down, since it is an institution dependent upon the existence of marriage, within which it affords a kind of safety-valve. Our present discussion, therefore, will move entirely within the framework of the bi-parental family considered as the rule.

Both Protestants and Catholics have, in general, viewed divorce not from the point of view of the biological purpose of the family, but from the point of view of the theological conception of sin. Catholics, since they hold that marriage is indissoluble in the sight of God, necessarily maintain that when two persons have once married, neither of them can, during the lifetime of the other, have sinless intercourse with any other person, no matter what may happen in the marriage. Protestants, in so far as they have favoured divorce, have done so partly out of opposition to Catholic doctrine on the sacraments, partly also because they perceived that the indissolubility of marriage is a cause of adultery, and they believed that easier divorce would make the diminution of adultery less difficult. One finds, accordingly, that in those Protestant countries where marriages are easily dissolved, adultery is viewed with extreme disfavour, while in countries which do not recognise divorce, adultery, though regarded as sinful, is winked at, at any rate where men are concerned. In Tsarist Russia, where divorce was exceedingly difficult, no one thought the worse of Gorki for his private life, whatever they may have thought of his politics. In America, on the contrary, where no one objected to his politics, he was hounded out on moral grounds, and no hotel would give him a night's lodging.

Neither the Protestant nor the Catholic point of view in

this matter can be upheld on rational grounds. Let us take the Catholic point of view first. Suppose that the husband or wife becomes insane after marriage; it is in this case not desirable that further children should spring from an insane stock, nor yet that any children who may already be born should be brought into contact with insanity. Complete separation of the parents, even supposing that the one who is insane has longer or shorter lucid intervals, is therefore desirable in the interests of the children. To decree that in this case the sane partner shall never be permitted any legally recognised sex relations is a wanton cruelty which serves no public purpose whatever. The sane partner is left with a very painful choice. He or she may decide in favour of continence, which is what the law and public morals expect; or in favour of surreptitious relations, presumably childless; or in favour of what is called open sin, with or without children. To each of these courses there are grave objections. Complete abstinence from sex, especially for one already accustomed to it in marriage, is very painful. It leads either a man or a woman, very often, to become prematurely old. It is not unlikely to produce nervous disorders, and in any case the effort involved tends to produce a disagreeable, grudging, and ill-tempered type of character. In a man, there is always a grave danger that his self-control will suddenly give way, leading him to acts of brutality, for if he is genuinely persuaded that all intercourse outside marriage is wicked, he is likely, if he does seek such intercourse, to feel that he might as well be hanged for a sheep as for a lamb, and therefore to throw off all moral restraints.

The second alternative, namely that of having surreptitious childless relations, is the one most commonly adopted in practice, in such a situation as we are considering. To this, also, there are grave objections. Everything surreptitious is undesirable, and sex relations which are serious cannot develop their best possibilities without children and a common life. Moreover, if a man or woman is young and vigorous, it is not in the public interest to say: 'You shall have no more children.' Still less is it to the public interest to say what the law does in fact say, namely: 'You shall have no more children unless you choose a lunatic for their other parent.'

The third alternative, namely that of living in 'open sin', is the one which is least harmful, both to the individual and to the community, where it is feasible, but for economic reasons it is impossible in most cases. A doctor or a lawyer who attempted to live in open sin would lose all his patients or clients. A man engaged in any branch of the scholastic profession would lose his post at once.[1] Even if economic circumstances do not make open sin impossible, most people will be deterred by the social penalties. Men like to belong to clubs, and women like to be respected and called on by other women. To be deprived of these pleasures is apparently considered a great hardship. Consequently open sin is difficult except for the rich, and for artists and writers and others whose profession makes it easy to live in a more or less bohemian society.

It follows that in any country which refuses divorce for insanity, as England does, the man or woman whose wife or husband becomes insane is placed in an intolerable position, in favour of which there is no argument whatever except theological superstition. And what is true of insanity is true also of venereal disease, habitual crime, and habitual drunkenness. All these are things which destroy a marriage from every point of view. They make companionship impossible, procreation undesirable, and association of the guilty parent with the child a thing to be avoided. In such cases, therefore, divorce can only be opposed on the ground that marriage is a trap by which the unwary are tricked into purification through sorrow.

Desertion, when it is genuine, should, of course, be a

[1] Unless he happens to teach at one of the older universities and to be closely related to a peer who has been a Cabinet Minister.

ground for divorce, for in that case the decree merely recognises in law what is already the fact, namely that the marriage
is at an end. From a legal point of view, however, there is the
awkwardness that desertion, if it is a ground for divorce, will
be resorted to for that reason, and will be therefore far more
frequent than it would be if it were not such a ground. The
same kind of difficulty arises in regard to various causes which
are in themselves perfectly valid. Many married couples have
such a passionate desire to part that they will resort to almost
any expedient allowed by the law. When, as was the case in
England formerly, a man had to be guilty of cruelty as well as
adultery in order to be divorced, it not infrequently happened
that a husband would arrange with his wife to hit her before
the servants, in order that evidence of cruelty might be forth-
coming. Whether it is altogether desirable that two people
who passionately desire to part should be forced to endure
each other's companionship by the pressure of the law is
another question. But we must in all fairness recognise that
whatever grounds of divorce are allowed will be stretched to
the uttermost, and that many people will purposely behave in
such a manner as to make these grounds available. Let us,
however, neglecting legal difficulties, continue our inquiry
into the circumstances which in fact make the persistence of a
marriage undesirable.

Adultery in itself should not, to my mind, be a ground of
divorce. Unless people are restrained by inhibitions or strong
moral scruples, it is very unlikely that they will go through life
without occasionally having strong impulses to adultery. But
such impulses do not by any means necessarily imply that the
marriage no longer serves its purpose. There may still be
ardent affection between husband and wife, and every desire
that the marriage should continue. Suppose, for example, that
a man has to be away from home on business for a number of
months on end. If he is physically vigorous, he will find it
difficult to remain continent throughout this time, however

fond he may be of his wife. The same will apply to his wife, if she is not entirely convinced of the correctness of conventional morality. Infidelity in such circumstances ought to form no barrier whatever to subsequent happiness, and in fact it does not, where the husband and wife do not consider it necessary to indulge in melodramatic orgies of jealousy. We may go farther, and say that each party should be able to put up with such temporary fancies as are always liable to occur, provided the underlying affection remains intact. The psychology of adultery has been falsified by conventional morals, which assume, in monogamous countries, that attraction to one person cannot co-exist with a serious affection for another. Everybody knows that this is untrue, yet everybody is liable, under the influence of jealousy, to fall back upon this untrue theory, and make mountains out of molehills. Adultery, therefore, is no good ground for divorce, except when it involves a deliberate preference for another person, on the whole, to the husband or the wife, as the case may be.

In saying this I am, of course, assuming that the adulterous intercourse will not be such as to lead to children. Where illegitimate children come in, the issue is much more complicated. This is especially the case if the children are those of the wife, for in that case, if the marriage persists, the husband is faced with the necessity of having another man's child brought up with his own, and (if scandal is to be avoided) even as his own. This goes against the biological basis of marriage, and will also involve an almost intolerable instinctive strain. On this ground, in the days before contraceptives, adultery perhaps deserved the importance which was attached to it, but contraceptives have made it far more possible than it formerly was to distinguish sexual intercourse as such from marriage as a procreative partnership. On this ground it is now possible to attach much less importance to adultery than is attached to it in the conventional code.

The grounds which may make divorce desirable are of two

kinds. There are those due to the defects of one partner, such as insanity, dipsomania, and crime; and there are those based upon the relations of the husband and wife. It may happen that, without blame to either party, it is impossible for a married couple to live together amicably, or without some very grave sacrifice. It may happen that each has important work to do, and that the work requires that they should live in different places. It may happen that one of them, without disliking the other, becomes deeply attached to some other person, so deeply as to feel the marriage an intolerable tie. In that case, if there is no legal redress, hatred is sure to spring up. Indeed, such cases, as everyone knows, are quite capable of leading to murder. Where a marriage breaks down owing to incompatibility or to an overwhelming passion on the part of one partner for some other person, there should not be, as there is at present, a determination to attach blame. For this reason, much the best ground of divorce in all such cases is mutual consent. Grounds other than mutual consent ought only to be required where the marriage has failed through some definite defect in one partner.

There is very great difficulty in framing laws as regards divorce, because whatever the laws may be, judges and juries will be governed by their passions, while husbands and wives will do whatever may be necessary to circumvent the intentions of the legislators. Although in English law a divorce cannot be obtained where there is any agreement between husband and wife, yet everybody knows that in practice there often is such an agreement. In New York State it is not uncommon to go farther and hire perjured testimony to prove the statutory adultery. Cruelty is in theory a perfectly adequate ground for divorce, but it may be interpreted so as to become absurd. When the most eminent of all film-stars was divorced by his wife for cruelty, one of the counts in the proof of cruelty was that he used to bring home friends who talked about Kant. I can hardly suppose that it was the intention of the California legislators to enable any woman to divorce her husband on the ground that he was sometimes guilty of intelligent conversation in her presence. The only way out of these confusions, subterfuges, and absurdities is to have divorce by mutual consent in all cases where there is not some very definite and demonstrable reason, such as insanity, to justify a onesided desire for divorce. The parties would then have to settle all monetary adjustments out of court, and it would not be necessary for either party to hire clever men to prove the other a monster of iniquity. I should add that nullity, which is now decreed where sexual intercourse is impossible, should instead be granted on application whenever the marriage is childless. That is to say, if a husband and wife who have no children wish to part, they should be able to do so on production of a medical certificate to the effect that the wife is not pregnant. Children are the purpose of marriage, and to hold people to a childless marriage is a cruel cheat.

So much for the *law* of divorce; the *custom* is another matter. As we have already seen, it is possible for the law to make divorce easy while, nevertheless, custom makes it rare. The great frequency of divorce in America comes, I think, partly from the fact that what people seek in marriage is not what should be sought, and this in turn is due partly to the fact that adultery is not tolerated. Marriage should be a partnership intended by both parties to last at least as long as the youth of their children, and not regarded by either as at the mercy of temporary amours. If such temporary amours are not tolerated by public opinion or by the consciences of those concerned, each in its turn has to blossom into a marriage. This may easily go so far as completely to destroy the biparental family, for if a woman has a fresh husband every two years, and a fresh child by each, the children in effect are deprived of their fathers, and marriage therefore loses its *raison d'être*. We come back again to St Paul: marriage in

America, as in the First Epistle to the Corinthians, is conceived as an alternative to fornication; therefore whenever a man would fornicate if he could not get a divorce, he must have a divorce.

When marriage is conceived in relation to children, a quite different ethic comes into play. Thus husband and wife, if they have any love for their children, will so regulate their conduct as to give their children the best chance of a happy and healthy development. This may involve, at times, very considerable self-repression. And it certainly requires that both should realise the superiority of the claims of children to the claims of their own romantic emotions. But all this will happen of itself, and quite naturally, where parental affection is genuine and a false ethic does not inflame jealousy. There are some who say that if a husband and wife no longer love each other passionately, and do not prevent each other from sexual experiences outside marriage, it is impossible for them to co-operate adequately in the education of their children. Thus Mr Walter Lippmann says: 'Mates who are not lovers will not really co-operate, as Mr Bertrand Russell thinks they should, in bearing children; they will be distracted, insufficient, and worst of all, they will be merely dutiful.'[1] There is here, first of all, a minor, possibly unintentional, misstatement. Of course mates who are not lovers will not co-operate in *bearing* children; but children are not done with when they are born, as Mr Walter Lippmann seems to imply. And to co-operate in *rearing* children, even after passionate love has decayed is by no means a superhuman task for sensible people who are capable of the natural affections. To this I can testify from a large number of cases personally known to me. To say that such parents will be 'merely dutiful' is to ignore the emotion of parental affection – an emotion which, where it is genuine and strong, preserves an unbreakable tie between husband and wife long after physical passion has

[1] *Preface to Morals*, 1929, p. 308.

decayed. One must suppose that Mr Lippmann has never heard of France, where the family is strong, and parents very dutiful, in spite of an exceptional freedom in the matter of adultery. Family feeling is extremely weak in America, and the frequency of divorce is a consequence of this fact. Where family feeling is strong, divorce will be comparatively rare, even if it is legally easy. Easy divorce, as it exists in America, must be regarded as a transitional stage on the way from the bi-parental to the purely maternal family. It is, however, a stage involving considerable hardship for children, since in the world as it is, children expect to have two parents, and may become attached to their father before divorce takes place. So long as the bi-parental family continues to be the recognised rule, parents who divorce each other, except for grave cause, appear to me to be failing in their parental duty. I do not think that a legal compulsion to go on being married is likely to mend matters. What seems to me to be wanted is first, a degree of mutual liberty which will make marriage more endurable, and secondly, a realisation of the importance of children, which has been overlaid by the emphasis on sex which we owe to St Paul and the Romantic Movement.

The conclusion seems to be that, while divorce is too difficult in many countries, of which England is one, easy divorce does not afford a genuine solution of the marriage problem. If marriage is to continue, stability in marriage is important in the interests of the children, but this stability will be best sought by distinguishing between marriage and merely sexual relations, and by emphasising the biological as opposed to the romantic aspect of married love. I do not pretend that marriage can be freed from onerous duties. In the system which I commend, men are freed, it is true, from the duty of sexual conjugal fidelity, but they have in exchange the duty of controlling jealousy. The good life cannot be lived without self-control, but it is better to control a restrictive and hostile emotion such as jealousy, rather than a generous and expansive emotion such as love. Conventional morality has erred, not in demanding self-control, but in demanding it in the wrong place.

Chapter 17

Population

The main purpose of marriage is to replenish the human population of the globe. Some marriage systems perform this task inadequately, some too adequately. It is from this point of view that I wish to consider sexual morality in the present chapter.

In a state of nature, the larger mammals require a considerable area per head to keep themselves alive. Consequently, the total population of any species of large wild mammal is small. The population of sheep and cows is considerable, but that is due to human agency. The population of human beings is quite out of proportion to that of any other large mammal. This, of course, is due to our skill. The invention of bows and arrows, the domestication of ruminants, the beginnings of agriculture, and the industrial revolution, all of them increased the number of persons who could subsist on a square mile. The last of these economic advances, as we know from statistics, was utilised for this purpose; in all likelihood the others were also. Man's intelligence has been employed more to increase his numbers than for any other single purpose.

It is true that, as Mr Carr Saunders has pointed out, the usual rule has been for population to be practically stationary, and an increase such as has occurred in the nineteenth century is a most exceptional phenomenon. We may suppose that something similar occurred in Egypt and Babylonia when they took to irrigation and careful agriculture. But in historical times there seems to have been nothing of the sort. All estimates of population before the nineteenth century are very conjectural, but in this matter they all concur. A rapidly increasing population is, therefore, a rare and exceptional phenomenon. If, as seems to be the case, the population is now again tending to become stationary in the most civilised countries, that only means that they have worked through an abnormal condition and reverted to the usual practice of mankind.

The great merit of Mr Carr Saunders's book on population consists in its pointing out that voluntary restriction has been practised in almost all ages and places, and has been more effective in preserving a stationary population than elimination through a high mortality. Possibly he somewhat overstates his case. In India and China, for example, it seems to be mainly the high death-rate which prevents the population from increasing very rapidly. In China statistics are lacking, but in India they exist. The birth-rate there is enormous, yet the population, as Mr Carr Saunders himself points out, increases slightly more slowly than that of England. This is due mainly to infant mortality and plague and other grave diseases. I believe that China would show a similar state of affairs if statistics were available. In spite of these important exceptions, however, Mr Carr Saunders's thesis is undoubtedly true in the main. Various methods if limiting population have been practised. The simplest of these is infanticide, which has existed on a very large scale wherever religion has permitted it. Sometimes the practice has had such a firm hold that in accepting Christianity men have stipulated that it should not interfere with infanticide.[1] The Dukhobors, who got into trouble with the Tsarist Government for their refusal of military service on the ground that human life is sacred, subsequently got into trouble with the Canadian Government for their tendency to the practice of infanticide. Other methods have, however, also been common. Among many races, a

---

[1] This happened, for example, in Iceland. Carr Saunders, *Population*, 1925, p. 19.

woman abstains from sexual intercourse not only during pregnancy, but during lactation, which is often prolonged for two or three years. This necessarily limits her fertility very considerably, especially among savages, who grow old much sooner than civilised races. The Australian aborigines practise an exceedingly painful operation which very much diminishes male potency and restricts fertility in a marked degree. As we know from Genesis,[1] at least one definite birth-control method was known and practised in antiquity, although it was disapproved of by the Jews, whose religion was always very anti-Malthusian. By the use of these various devices, men escaped the wholesale deaths from starvation which would have occurred if they had used their fecundity to the utmost.

Starvation has, nevertheless, played a considerable part in keeping population down; not so much, perhaps, under quite primitive conditions as among agricultural peasant communities of a not very advanced type. The famine in Ireland in 1846-7 was so severe that the population has never since attained anything like the level that it had reached before. Famines in Russia have been frequent, and that of 1921 is still fresh in the memory of everyone. When I was in China in 1920, considerable portions of that country were suffering a famine quite as severe as the Russian famine of the following year, but the victims secured less sympathy than those of the Volga, because their misfortunes could not be attributed to Communism. Such facts show that population does sometimes increase up to and even beyond the limit of subsistence. This happens, however, especially where fluctuations are liable to diminish the amount of food suddenly and drastically.

Christianity, wherever it was believed, put an end to all checks upon the growth of population except continence. Infanticide was, of course, forbidden; so was abortion; and so

[1] Gen. xxxviii. 9, 10.

were all contraceptive measures. It is true that the clergy and the monks and nuns were celibate, but I do not suppose that in medieval Europe they formed so large a percentage of the population as unmarried women do in England at the present day. They did not, therefore, represent any statistically very important check upon fertility. Accordingly, in the Middle Ages, as compared with ancient times, there was probably a larger number of deaths caused by destitution and pestilence. The population increased very slowly. A slightly higher rate of increase marked the eighteenth century, but with the nineteenth century a quite extraordinary change took place, and the rate of growth reached a height which it had probably never attained before. It is estimated that in 1066 England and Wales contained 26 persons per square mile. In 1801 this figure had risen to 153; in 1901 it had risen to 561. The absolute increase during the nineteenth century is thus nearly four times as great as the increase from the Norman Conquest to the beginning of the nineteenth century. Nor does the increase of the population of England and Wales give an adequate picture of the facts, for during that period the British stock was peopling large parts of the world previously inhabited by a few savages.

There is very little reason to attribute this increase of population to an increase in the birth-rate. It is attributable rather to a decline in the death-rate, due partly to the advance of medical science, but much more, I think, to the rising level of prosperity brought about by the industrial revolution. From the year 1841, when the birth-rate began to be recorded in England, down to the years 1871-5, the birth-rate was nearly constant, reaching, in the latter period, a maximum of 35.5. At this stage two events occurred. The first was the Education Act of 1870; the second, the prosecution of Bradlaugh for neo-Malthusian propaganda in 1878. One finds, accordingly, that the birth-rate declined from that moment onward, at first slowly and then catastrophically.

The Education Act began to afford the motive, since children were no longer such a lucrative investment; and Bradlaugh afforded the means. In the quinquennial period 1911-15, the birth-rate had fallen to 23.6. In the first quarter of 1929, it had fallen to 16·5. The population of England is still slowly increasing owing to improvements in medicine and hygiene, but it is rapidly approaching a stationary figure.[1] France, as everyone knows, has had a virtually stationary population for a considerable time.

The fall in the birth-rate has been very rapid and nearly universal throughout Western Europe. The only exceptions have been backward countries such as Portugal. It has been more marked in urban than in rural communities. It began among the well-to-do, but has now penetrated to all classes in towns and industrial areas. The birth-rate is still higher among the poor than among the well-to-do, but it is lower now in the poorest boroughs of London than it was ten years ago in the richest. This fall, as everyone knows (although some will not admit it), is due to the use of contraceptives and abortion. There is no particular reason why it should stop at the point where it produces a stationary population. It may easily go on until the population begins to diminish, and the ultimate result may, for aught we can tell, be a virtual extinction of the most civilised races.

Before we can profitably discuss this problem, it is necessary to be clear as to what we desire. There is in any given state of economic technique what Carr Saunders calls an optimum density of population, that is to say, a density which gives the maximum income per head. If the population falls below this level or rises above it, the general level of economic well-being is diminished. Broadly speaking every advance in economic technique increases the optimum density of population. In the hunting stage, one person per square mile is

[1] In the first quarter of 1929 it diminished, but this is to be attributed to the influenza epidemic. See *Times*, May 27, 1929.

about right, whereas in an advanced industrial country a population of several hundred per square mile is likely to be not excessive. There is reason to think that England, since the war, is over-populated. One cannot say the same of France, still less of America. But it is not likely that France, or indeed any country of Western Europe, would *gain* in average wealth by an increase of population. That being so, we have no reason, from an economic point of view, to desire that population should increase. Those who feel this desire are usually inspired by motives of nationalistic militarism, and the increase of population that they desire is not to be a permanent one, since it is to be wiped out as soon as they can get the war at which they are aiming. In fact, therefore, the position of these people is that it is better to restrict population by death on the battlefield than by contraceptives. This view is not one which can be entertained by anyone who has thought it out, and those who seem to hold it do so only from muddleheadedness. Apart from arguments concerned with war, we have every reason to rejoice that the knowledge of birth-control methods is causing the population of civilised countries to become stationary.

The matter would, however, be quite otherwise if the population were actually to diminish, for a diminution, if it continues unchecked, means ultimate extinction, and we cannot desire to see the most civilised races of the world disappear. The use of contraceptives therefore, is only to be welcomed if steps can be taken to confine it within such limits as will preserve the population at about its present level. I do not think there is any difficulty in this. The motives to family limitation are mainly, though not wholly, economic, and the birth-rate could be increased by diminishing the expense of children, or, if this should prove necessary, by making them an actual source of income to their parents. Any such measure, however, in the present nationalistic world, would be very dangerous, since it would be used as a method of securing military preponderance. One can imagine all the leading military nations adding to the race of armaments a race of propagation, under the slogan: 'The cannon must have their fodder.' Here, again, we are faced with the absolute necessity of an international Government if civilisation is to survive. Such a Government, if it is to be effective in preserving the peace of the world, must pass decrees limiting the rate at which any military nation may increase its population. The hostility between Australia and Japan illustrates the gravity of this problem. The population of Japan increases very fast and that of Australia (apart from immigration) rather slowly. This causes a hostility which is exceedingly difficult to deal with, since apparently just principles can be appealed to by both sides in the dispute. It may, I think, be assumed that before very long throughout Western Europe and America the birth-rate will be such as to involve no increase in population, unless definite steps are taken by Governments with that end in view. But it cannot be expected that the most powerful military nations will sit still while other nations reverse the balance of power by the mere process of breeding. Any international authority which is to do its work properly will therefore be obliged to take the population question into consideration and to insist upon birth-control propaganda in any recalcitrant nation. Unless this is done, the peace of the world cannot be secure.

The population question is thus twofold. We have to guard against too rapid an increase of population, and we have also to guard against a decrease. The former danger is old, and exists in many countries such as Portugal, Spain, Russia, and Japan. The latter danger is new, and exists as yet only in Western Europe. It would exist also in America if America depended for its population upon breeding alone, but hitherto immigration has caused the population of America to increase at least as fast as is desirable, in spite of a very low birth-rate among native-born Americans. The new danger, that of a dwindling population, is one to which our ancestral habits of thought are not adapted. It has been met by moral homilies and by laws against birth-control propaganda. Such methods, as the statistics show, are quite unavailing. The use of contraceptives has become part of the common practice of all civilised nations, and cannot now be eradicated. The habit of not facing facts where sex is concerned is so deeply rooted in Governments and important persons that it cannot be expected to cease suddenly. It is, however, a very undesirable habit, and I think it may be hoped that, when those who are now young acquire positions of importance, they will be better in this respect than their fathers and grandfathers. One may hope that they will frankly recognise the inevitability of contraceptive practices, and their desirability so long as they do not cause an actual diminution of population. The proper course in any nation which is threatened with an actual decrease is obviously an experimental diminution of the financial burden of children until the point is reached where the birth-rate is such as to maintain the existing population.

In this connection there is one respect in which our existing moral code might be altered with advantage. There are in England some two million more women than men, and these are condemned by law and custom to remain childless, which is undoubtedly to many of them a great deprivation. If custom tolerated the unmarried mother, and made her economic situation tolerable, it cannot be doubted that a great many of the women at present condemned to celibacy would have children. Strict monogamy is based upon the assumption that the numbers of the sexes will be approximately equal. Where this is not the case, it involves considerable cruelty to those whom arithmetic compels to remain single. And where there is reason to desire an increase in the birth-rate, this cruelty may be publicly as well as privately undesirable.

As knowledge increases, it becomes more and more possible to control, by deliberate Governmental action, forces which hitherto have seemed like forces of nature. Increase of population is one of these. Since the introduction of Christianity, it has been left to the blind operation of instinct. But the time is rapidly approaching when it will have to be deliberately controlled. In this matter, however, as before in regard to the State control of childhood, we have found that State interference, if it is to be beneficial, will have to be the interference of an international State, not of the competing militaristic States of the present day.

Chapter 18

Eugenics

Eugenics is the attempt to improve the biological character of a breed by deliberate methods adopted to that end. The ideas upon which it is based are Darwinian, and, appropriately enough, the President of the Eugenics Society is a son of Charles Darwin; but the more immediate progenitor of eugenic ideas was Francis Galton, who strongly emphasised the hereditary factor in human achievement. In our day, especially in America, heredity has become a party question. American Conservatives maintain that the finished character of a grown man is mainly due to congenital characteristics, while American Radicals maintain, on the contrary, that education is everything and heredity nothing. I cannot agree with either of these two extreme positions, nor with the premise which they share and which gives rise to their opposite prejudices, namely that Italians, South Slavs, and such are inferior, as finished products, to the native-born American of the Ku Klux Klan. No data exist as yet for determining, in regard to human mental capacity, what part is due to heredity and what to education. If the matter were to be scientifically determined, it would be necessary to take thousands of pairs of identical twins, separate them at birth, and educate them in ways as widely divergent as possible. At present, however, this experiment is not practicable. My own belief, which I confess to be unscientific and based merely upon impressions, is that, while anybody can be ruined by a bad education, and in fact almost everybody is, only people with certain native aptitudes can achieve great excellence in various directions. I do not believe that any degree of education would turn the average boy into a first-class pianist; I do not believe that the best school in the world could turn us all into Einsteins; I do not believe that Napoleon was not superior in native endowment to his school-fellows at Brienne, and had merely learned strategy through watching his mother manage her brood of unruly sons. I am convinced that in such cases, and to a lesser degree in all cases of ability, there is a native aptitude which causes education to produce better results than it does with average material. There are, indeed, obvious facts which point to this conclusion, such as that one can generally tell whether a man is a clever man or a fool by the shape of his head, which can hardly be regarded as a characteristic conferred by education. Then again, consider the opposite extreme, that of idiocy, imbecility, and feeblemindedness. Not even the most fanatical opponent of eugenics denies that idiocy is, at any rate in most cases, congenital, and to any person with a feeling for statistical symmetry, this implies that at the opposite end also there will be a corresponding percentage of persons with abnormally great capacity. I shall therefore assume without more ado that human beings differ in regard to congenital mental capacity. I shall assume also, what is perhaps more dubious, that clever people are preferable to their opposite. These two points being conceded, the foundations are laid for the eugenists' case. We must not, therefore, pooh-pooh the whole position, whatever we may think of some of the details in certain of its advocates.

There has been a quite exceptional lot of nonsense written on the subject of eugenics. Most of its advocates add to their sound biological foundation certain sociological propositions of a less indubitable nature. Such are: that virtue is proportional to income; that the inheritance of poverty (alas, too common) is a biological, not a legal phenomenon; and that, therefore, if we could induce the rich to breed instead of the poor, everybody would be rich. A great deal of fuss is made about the fact that the poor breed more than the rich. I cannot bring myself to regard this fact as very regrettable, since I see no evidence whatever that the rich are in any way superior to the poor. Even if it were regrettable, it would not be matter for very serious regret, since there is, in fact, only a lag of a few years. The birth-rate diminishes among the poor, and is quite as small now among them as it was nine years ago among the rich.[1] There are certain factors, it is true, which make for a differential birth-rate of an undesirable kind. For example, when Governments and police authorities place difficulties in the way of the acquisition of birth-control information, the result is that persons whose intelligence falls below a certain level fail to acquire this information, while with others the attempts of the authorities are unsuccessful. Consequently all opposition to the dissemination of knowledge concerning contraceptives leads to stupid people having larger families than intelligent ones. It seems probable, however, that this is a very temporary factor, since before long even the stupidest will have either acquired birth-control information or – what I fear is a tolerably common result of the obscurantism of the authorities – will have discovered persons willing to procure abortion.[2]

Eugenics is of two sorts, positive and negative. The former is concerned with the encouragement of good stocks, the latter with the discouragement of bad ones. The latter is at present more practicable. It has, indeed, made great strides in certain States in America, and the sterilisation of the unfit is within the scope of immediate practical politics in England. The objections to such a measure which one naturally feels

[1] See Julius Wolf, *Die neue Sexualmoral und das Geburtenproblem unserer Tage*, 1928, pp. 165–7.

[2] According to Julius Wolf (*op. cit.*, pp. 6 ff.), abortion plays a larger part than contraceptives in accounting for the fall of the birth-rate in Germany. He estimates that there are 600,000 artificial abortions annually in Germany at the present day. It is more difficult to arrive at an estimate for Great Britain, owing to the fact that miscarriages are not registered; but there is reason to think that the facts are not so very different from those in Germany.

are, I believe, not justified. Feeble-minded women, as every-one knows, are apt to have enormous numbers of illegitimate children, all, as a rule, wholly worthless to the community. These women would themselves be happier if they were ster-ilised, since it is not from any philoprogenitive impulse that they become pregnant. The same thing, of course, applies to feeble-minded men. There are, it is true, grave dangers in the system, since the authorities may easily come to consider any unusual opinion or any opposition to themselves a mark of feeble-mindedness. These dangers, however, are probably worth incurring, since it is quite clear that the number of idiots, imbeciles, and feeble-minded could, by such measures be enormously diminished.

Measures of sterilisation should, in my opinion, be very definitely confined to persons who are *mentally* defective. I cannot favour laws such as that of Idaho, which allows ster-ilisation of 'mental defectives, epileptics, habitual criminals, moral degenerates, and sex perverts.' The last two categories here are very vague, and will be determined differently in different communities. The law of Idaho would have justified the sterilisation of Socrates, Plato, Julius Caesar, and St Paul. Moreover, the habitual criminal may very possibly be the victim of some functional nervous disorder which could, at least theoretically, be cured by psycho-analysis, and which might well be not hereditary. Both in England and in America the laws on such subjects are framed in ignorance of the work of psycho-analysts, and they therefore lump together entirely different types of disorder, merely on the ground that they display somewhat similar symptoms. They are, that is to say, some thirty years behind the best knowledge of the time. This illustrates the fact that in all such matters it is very dangerous to legislate until science has arrived at stable conclusions which have remained unchallenged for several decades at least, since, otherwise, false ideas become embodied in stat-utes, and therefore endeared to magistrates, with the result that the practical application of better ideas is greatly retarded. Mental deficiency is, to my mind, the only thing at present sufficiently definite to be safely made the subject of legal enactment in this region. It can be decided in an objective manner, concerning which authorities would not disagree, whereas moral degeneracy, for example, is a matter of opinion. The same person whom one man might consider a moral degenerate will be considered by another to be a prophet. I do not say that the law ought not, at some future time, to be extended more widely – I say only that our scientific knowledge at present is not adequate for this purpose, and that it is very dangerous when a community allows its moral reprobations to masquerade in the guise of science, as has undoubtedly happened in various American States.

I come now to positive eugenics, which has more interesting possibilities, though as yet they belong to the future. Positive eugenics consists in the attempt to encourage desirable parents to have a large number of children. At present the exact contrary is general. An abnormally clever boy in an elementary school, for example, will rise into the professional classes, and will probably, therefore, marry at the age of thirty-five or forty, whereas those in his original environment who are not unusually clever will marry at about twenty-five. The expense of education is a grave burden in the professional classes, and therefore causes them to limit their families very severely. Probably their intellectual average is somewhat higher than that of most other classes, so that this limitation is regrettable. The simplest measure for dealing with their case would be to grant free education up to and including the university to their children. That is to say, broadly speaking, that scholarships should be awarded on the merits of the parents rather than of the children. This would have the incidental advantage of doing away with cramming and overwork, which at present causes most of the cleverest young people to be intellectually and physically damaged by too much strain before they reach the age of twenty-one. It would probably, however, be impossible, either in England or in America, for the State to adopt any measure really adequate to cause professional men to breed large families. What stands in the way is democracy. The ideas of eugenics are based on the assumption that men are unequal, while democracy is based on the assumption that they are equal. It is, therefore, politically very difficult to carry out eugenic ideas in a democratic community when those ideas take the form, not of suggesting that there is a minority of *inferior* people such as imbeciles, but of admitting that there is a minority of *superior* people. The former is pleasing to the majority, the latter unpleasing. Measures embodying the former fact can therefore win the support of a majority, while measures embodying the latter cannot.

Nevertheless, every person who has given any thought to the subject knows that, although at present it may be difficult to determine who constitutes the best stocks, yet undoubtedly there are differences in this respect which science may hope to be able to measure before long. Imagine the feelings of a farmer who was told that he must give all his bull calves an equal opportunity. As a matter of fact, the bull which is to be the progenitor of the next generation is very carefully selected for the milk-giving qualities of his female ancestors. (We may note in passing that since science, art, and war are unknown to this species, prominent merit attaches only to the female sex, and the male is at best a transmitter of feminine excellences.) All domestic animals have been improved enormously by scientific breeding, and it is not open to question that human beings could, by similar methods, be changed in any desired direction. It is, of course, much more difficult to determine what we desire in human beings. It may be that if we bred people for physical strength we should diminish their brains. It may be that if we bred them for mental capacity we should render them more liable to various diseases. It may be that if we sought to produce emotional balance we should destroy art. On all these matters the necessary knowledge does not exist. It is not, therefore, desirable to do much in the way of positive eugenics at the present time. But it may easily be that within the next hundred years the sciences of heredity and bio-chemistry will have made such strides as to make possible the breeding of a race which everybody would admit to be superior to that now existing.

To apply scentific knowledge of this sort, however, would demand a more radical upheaval as regards the family than anything hitherto contemplated in these pages. If scientific breeding is to be carried out thoroughly, it will be necessary to set apart in each generation some two or three per cent of the males and some twenty-five per cent of the females for the purpose of propagation. There will be, presumably at puberty, an examination, as a result of which all the unsuccessful candidates will be sterilised. The father will have no more connection with his offspring than a bull or stallion has at present, and the mother will be a specialised professional, distinguished from other women by her manner of life. I do not say that this state of affairs is going to come about, still less do I say that I desire it, for I confess that I find it exceedingly repugnant. Nevertheless, when the matter is examined objectively, it is seen that such a plan might produce remarkable results. Let us suppose, for the sake of argument, that it is adopted in Japan, and that at the end of three generations most Japanese men are as clever as Edison and as strong as a prize-fighter. If, meanwhile, the other nations of the world had continued to leave matters to nature, they would be quite unable to stand up against Japan in warfare. Doubtless the Japanese, having reached such a pitch of ability, would find ways of employing the men of some other nation as soldiers, and would rely upon their scientific technique for victory, which they would be pretty sure to achieve. In such a system, blind devotion to the State would be very easy to instil in youth. Can anyone say that a development of this sort in the future is impossible?

There is a kind of eugenics, very popular with certain types of politicians and publicists, which may be called race eugenics. This consists in the contention that one race or nation (of course that to which the writer belongs) is very superior to all others, and ought to use its military power to increase its numbers at the expense of inferior stocks. The most noteworthy example of this is the Nordic propaganda in the United States, which has succeeded in winning legislative recognition in the immigration laws. This kind of eugenics can appeal to the Darwinian principle of survival of the fittest; yet, oddly enough, its most ardent advocates are those who consider that the teaching of Darwinism should be illegal. The political propaganda bound up with racial eugenics is mostly of an undesirable sort; but let us forget this, and examine the question on its merits.

In extreme cases, there can be little doubt of the superiority of one race to another. North America, Australia, and New Zealand certainly contribute more to the civilisation of the world than they would do if they were still peopled by aborigines. There is no sound reason to regard negroes as on the average inferior to white men, although for work in the tropics they are indispensable, so that their extermination (apart from questions of humanity) would be highly undesirable. But when it comes to discriminating among the races of Europe, a mass of bad science has to be brought in to support political prejudice. Nor do I see any valid ground for regarding the yellow races as in any degree inferior to our noble selves. In all such cases, racial eugenics is merely an excuse for Chauvinism.

Julius Wolf[1] gives a table of the excess of births over deaths per 1,000 of the population if all the principal countries for which statistics exist. France is lowest (1.3), USA

[1] *Op. cit.*, pp. 143-4.

next (4.0), then Sweden (5.8), British India (5.9), Switzerland (6.2), England (6.2). Germany has 7.8, Italy 10.9, Japan 14.6, Russia 19.5, and Ecuador, which leads the world, 23.1. China does not appear in the list, since the facts are unknown. Wolf draws the conclusion that the Western world will be overwhelmed by the East, i.e. by Russia, China, and Japan. I shall not attempt to rebut his argument by pinning my faith on Ecuador. Rather I shall point to his figures (already referred to) for the relative birth-rates among rich and poor in London, showing that the latter are now lower than the former were a few years ago. The same thing, though with a longer time-interval, applies to the East: as it becomes Occidentalised, its birth-rate will inevitably fall. A country cannot become formidable in a military sense except by becoming industrialised, and industrialism brings with it the type of mentality that leads to family limitation. We are therefore forced to conclude, not only that the domination of the East, which Western Chauvinists (following the ex-Kaiser) profess to dread, would be no great misfortune if it occurred, but also that there is no valid ground for expecting that it will come about. Nevertheless, war-mongers will probably continue to use this bogy, among others, until such time as an international authority can assign the permissible quota of increase for the populations of the various States.

Here again, as on two former occasions, we are confronted by the dangers facing mankind if science advances while international anarchy continues. Science enables us to realise our purposes, and if our purposes are evil, the result is disaster. If the world remains filled with malevolence and hate, the more scientific it becomes the more horrible it will be. To diminish the virulence of these passions is, therefore, an essential of human progress. To a very great extent their existence has been brought about by a wrong sexual ethic and a bad sexual education. For the future of civilisation a new and better sexual ethic is indispensable. It is this fact that makes the reform of sexual morality one of the vital needs of our time.

From the standpoint of private morals, sexual ethics, if scientific and unsuperstitious, would accord the first place to eugenic considerations. That is to say that, however the existing restraints upon sexual intercourse might be relaxed, a conscientious man and woman would not enter upon procreation without the most serious considerations as to the probable value of their progeny. Contraceptives have made parenthood voluntary and no longer an automatic result of sexual intercourse. For various economic reasons which we have considered in earlier chapters, it seems likely that the father will have less importance in regard to the education and maintenance of children in the future than he has had in the past. There will therefore be no very cogent reason why a woman should choose as the father of her child the man whom she prefers as a lover or a companion. It may become quite easily possible for women in the future, without any serious sacrifice of happiness, to select the fathers of their children by eugenic considerations, while allowing their private feelings free sway as regards ordinary sexual companionship. For men it would be still easier to select the mothers of their children for their desirability as parents. Those who hold, as I do, that sexual behaviour concerns the community solely in so far as children are involved, must draw from this premise a twofold conclusion as regards the morality of the future. On the one hand, that love apart from children should be free, but on the other hand, that the procreation of children should be a matter far more carefully regulated by moral considerations than it is at present. The considerations involved will, however, be somewhat different from those hitherto recognised. In order that procreation in a given case may be regarded as virtuous, it will no longer be necessary that certain words should have been pronounced by a priest, or a certain document drawn up by a registrar, for there is no evidence that such acts affect the health or intelligence of the offspring.

What will be considered necessary is that the given man and woman, in themselves and in the heredity which they transmit, should be such as are likely to have desirable children. When science becomes able to pronounce on this question with more certainty than is possible at present, the moral sense of the community may come to be more exacting from a eugenic point of view. The men with the best heredity may come to be eagerly sought after as fathers, while other men, though they may be acceptable as lovers, may find themselves rejected when they aim at paternity. The institution of marriage, as it has existed hitherto, has made any such schemes contrary to human nature, so that the practical possibilities of eugenics have been thought to be very restricted. But there is no reason to suppose that human nature will in future interpose a similar barrier, since contraceptives are separating procreation from childless sexual relations, and fathers are likely in future to have no such personal relation with their children as they have had in the past. The seriousness and the high social purpose which moralists in the past have attached to marriage will, if the world becomes more scientific in its ethics, attach only to procreation.

This eugenic outlook, although it must begin as the private ethic of certain unusually scientific people, is likely to grow more and more widespread, until at last it comes to be embodied in the law, presumably in the form of pecuniary rewards to desirable parents, and pecuniary penalties to such as are undesirable.

The idea of allowing science to interfere with our intimate personal impulses is undoubtedly repugnant. But the interference involved would be much less than that which has been tolerated for ages on the part of religion. Science is new in the world, and has not yet that authority due to tradition and early influence that religion has over most of us; but it is perfectly capable of acquiring the same authority and of being submitted to with the same degree of acquiescence that has characterised men's attitude towards religious precepts. The welfare of posterity is, it is true, a motive by no means sufficient to control the average man in his passionate moments, but if it became a part of recognised positive morality, with the sanction not only of praise and blame but of economic rewards and penalties, it would soon come to be accepted as a consideration which no well-conducted person could afford to ignore. Religion has existed since before the dawn of history, while science has existed for at most four centuries; but when science has become old and venerable, it will control our lives as much as religion has ever done. I foresee the time when all who care for the freedom of the human spirit will have to rebel against a scientific tyranny. Nevertheless, if there is to be a tyranny, it is better that it should be scientific.

Chapter 19

Sex and Individual Well-being

In the present chapter I propose to recapitulate things said in earlier chapters as regards the effects of sex and sexual morals upon individual happiness and well-being. In this matter we are not concerned only with the actively sexual period of life, nor with actual sex relations. Sexual morality affects childhood, adolescence, and even old age, in all kinds of ways, good or bad according to circumstances.

Conventional morality begins its operations by the imposition of taboos in childhood. A child is taught, at a very early age, not to touch certain parts of the body while grown-up people are looking. It is taught to speak in a whisper when expressing an excretory desire, and to preserve privacy in performing the resulting action. Certain parts of the body and certain acts have some peculiar quality not readily intelligible to the child, which invests them with mystery and a special interest. Certain intellectual problems, such as where babies come from, must be thought over in silence, since the answers given by grown-ups are either evasive or obviously untrue. I know men, by no means old, who, when in infancy they were seen touching a certain portion of their body, were told with the utmost solemnity: 'I would rather see you dead than doing that.' I regret to say that the effect in producing virtue in later life has not always been all that conventional moralists might desire. Not infrequently threats are used. It is perhaps not so common as it used to be to threaten a child with castration, but it is still thought quite proper to threaten him with insanity.

Indeed, it is illegal in the State of New York to let him know that he does not run this risk unless he thinks he does. The result of this teaching is that most children in their earliest years have a profound sense of guilt and terror which is associated with sexual matters. This association of sex with guilt and fear goes so deep as to become almost or wholly unconscious. I wish it were possible to institute a statistical inquiry, among men who believe themselves emancipated from such nursery tales, as to whether they would be as ready to commit adultery during a thunderstorm as at any other time. I believe that ninety per cent of them, in their heart of hearts, would think that if they did so they would be struck by lightning.

Both sadism and masochism, although in their milder forms they are normal, are connected, in their pernicious manifestations, with the sense of sexual guilt. A masochist is a man acutely conscious of his own guilt in connection with sex. A sadist is a man more conscious of the guilt of the woman as temptress. These effects, in later life, show how profound has been the early impression produced by unduly severe moral teaching in childhood. On this matter, persons connected with the teaching of children, and especially with the care of the very young, are becoming more enlightened. But unfortunately enlightenment has not yet reached the law-courts.

Childhood and youth form a period in life when pranks and naughtiness and performances of forbidden acts are natural, spontaneous, and not regrettable except when carried too far. But infraction of sex prohibitions is treated by grown-up people quite differently from any other breach of rules, and is therefore felt by the child to belong to a quite different category. If a child steals fruit from the larder you may be annoyed, you may rate the child soundly, but you feel no moral horror, and you do not convey to the child the sense that something appalling has occurred. If, on the other hand, you are an old-fashioned person and you find him masturbating, there will be a tone in your voice which he will never hear in any other connection. This tone produces an abject terror, all the greater since the child probably finds it impossible to abstain from the behaviour that has called forth your denunciation. The child, impressed by your earnestness, profoundly believes that masturbation is as wicked as you say it is. Nevertheless, he persists in it. Thus the foundations are laid for a morbidness which probably continues through life. From his earliest youth onward, he regards himself as a sinner. He soon learns to sin in secret, and to find a half-hearted consolation in the fact that no one knows of his sin. Being profoundly unhappy, he seeks to avenge himself on the world by punishing those who have been less successful than himself in concealing a similar guilt. Being accustomed to deceit as a child, he find no difficulty in practising it in later life. Thus he becomes a morbidly introverted hypocrite and persecutor as a result of his parents' ill-judged attempt to make him what they consider virtuous.

It is not guilt and shame and fear that should dominate the lives of children. Children should be happy and gay and spontaneous; they should not dread their own impulses; they should not shrink away from the exploration of natural facts. They should not hide away in the darkness all their instinctive life. They should not bury in the depths of the unconscious impulses which, even with their utmost endeavours, they cannot kill. If they are to grow into upright men and women, intellectually honest, socially fearless, vigorous in action and tolerant in thought, we must begin from the very beginning to train them so that these results may be possible. Education has been conceived too much on the anology of the training of dancing bears. Everyone knows how dancing bears are trained. They are put on a hot floor, which compels them to dance because their toes are burnt if they remain in contact with it. While this is done, a certain tune is played to them. After a time the tune suffices to make them dance, without the hot floor. So it is with children. While a child is conscious of his sexual organ, grown-ups scold him. In the end, such consciousness brings up a thought of their scolding and makes him dance to their tune, to the complete destruction of all possibility of a healthy or happy sexual life.

In the next stage, that of adolescence, the misery caused by the conventional handling of sex is even greater than in childhood. Many boys do not know at all accurately what is happening to them, and are terrified when they first experience nocturnal emissions. They find themselves filled with impulses which they have been taught to consider extremely wicked. These impulses are so strong as to be an obsession, day and night. In the better sort of boy, there are at the same time impulses of the most extreme idealism towards beauty and poetry, and towards ideal love, which is thought of as wholly divorced from sex. Owing to the Manichaean elements in Christian teaching, the idealistic and the carnal impulses of adolescence are apt, among ourselves, to remain wholly dissociated, and even at war one with the other. On this point I may quote the confession of an intellectual friend, who says: 'My own adolescence was, I believe, not untypical, and it exhibited this dissociation in a very marked form. For hours in the day I would read Shelley and sentimentalise over:

> The desire of the moth for the star,
> Of the night for the morrow.

Then suddenly I would leave these heights and try to catch a surreptitious glimpse of the housemaid undressing. The latter impulse caused me profound shame; the former had, of course, an element of silliness, since its idealism was the obverse of a foolish fear of sex.'

Adolescence, as everyone knows, is a time when nervous disorders are very frequent, and when persons who at all other times are well balanced may easily be quite the reverse. Miss Mead, in her book called *Coming of Age in Samoa*, asserts that adolescent disorders are unknown in that island,

and she attributes this fact to the prevalent sexual freedom.[1]
This sexual freedom, it is true, is being somewhat curtailed by
missionary activity. Some of the girls whom she questioned
lived in the missionary's house, and these, during adolescence, practised only masturbation and homosexuality,
whilst those who lived elsewhere engaged also in heterosexual
practices. Our most famous boys' schools are not altogether so
very different in this respect from the house of the Samoan
missionary, but the psychological effect of behaviour which,
in Samoa, is harmless, may in an English schoolboy be disastrous, because he probably respects in his heart the conventional teaching, whereas the Samoan regards the
missionary merely as a white man with peculiar tastes that
have to be humoured.

Most young men, in their early adult years, go through
troubles and difficulties of a quite unnecessary kind in regard
to sex. If a young man remains chaste, the difficulty of control
probably causes him to become timid and inhibited, so that
when he finally marries he cannot break down the self-control
of past years, except perhaps in a brutal and sudden manner,
which leads him to fail his wife in the capacity of a lover. If he
goes with prostitutes, the dissociation between the physical
and the idealistic aspects of love which has begun in adolescence is perpetuated, with the result that his relations with
women ever after have to be either platonic or, in his belief,
degrading. Moreover, he runs a grave risk of venereal disease.
If he has affairs with girls of his own class, much less harm is
done, but even then the need of secrecy is harmful, and interferes with the development of stable relations. Owing partly
to snobbery and partly to the belief that marriage ought immediately to lead to children, it is difficult for a man to marry
young. Moreover, where divorce is very difficult, early marriage has great dangers, since two people who suit each other
at twenty are quite likely not to suit each other at thirty.

[1] p. 157.

Stable relations with one partner are difficult for many people until they have had some experience of variety. If our outlook on sex were sane, we should expect university students to be temporarily married though childless. They would in this way be freed from the obsession of sex, which at present greatly interferes with work. They would acquire that experience of the other sex which is desirable as a prelude to the serious partnership of a marriage with children. And they would be free to experience love without the concomitants of subterfuge, concealment, and dread of disease which at present poison youthful adventures.

For the large class of women who, as things are, must remain permanently unmarried, conventional morality is painful and, in most cases, harmful. I have known, as we all have, unmarried women of strict conventional virtue who deserve the highest admiration from every possible point of view. But I think the general rule is otherwise. A woman who has had no experience of sex and has considered it important to preserve her virtue has been engaged in a negative reaction, tinged with fear, and has therefore, as a rule, become timid, while at the same time instinctive unconscious jealousy has filled her with disapproval of normal people, and with a desire to punish those who have enjoyed what she has foregone. Intellectual timidity is an especially common concomitant of prolonged virginity. Indeed, I am inclined to think that the intellectual inferiority of women, in so far as it exists, is mainly due to the restraint upon curiosity which the fear of sex leads them to impose. There is no good reason for the unhappiness and waste involved in the lifelong virginity of these women who cannot find an exclusive husband. The present situation, in which this necessarily occurs very frequently, was not contemplated in the earlier days of the institution of marriage, since in those days the numbers of the sexes were approximately equal. Undoubtedly, the existence of a great excess of women in many countries affords a very serious argument in favour of modifications of the conventional moral code.

Marriage, the one conventionally tolerated outlet for sex, itself suffers from the rigidity of the code. The complexes acquired in childhood, the experiences of men with prostitutes, and the attitude of aversion from sex instilled into young ladies in order to preserve their virtue, all militate against happiness in marriage. A well-brought-up girl, if her sexual impulses are strong, will be unable to distinguish, when she is courted, between a serious congeniality with a man and mere sex attraction. She may easily marry the first man who awakens her sexually, and find out too late that when her sexual hunger is satisfied she has no longer anything in common with him. Everything has been done in the education of the two to make her unduly timid and him unduly sudden in the sexual approach. Neither has the knowledge on sexual matters that each ought to have, and very often initial failures, due to this ignorance, make the marriage ever after sexually unsatisfying to both. Moreover mental as well as physical companionship is rendered difficult. A woman is not accustomed to free speech on sexual matters. A man is not accustomed to it, except with men and prostitutes. In the most intimate and vital concern of their mutual life, they are shy, awkward, even wholly silent. The wife, perhaps, lies awake unsatisfied and hardly knowing what it is she wants. The man, perhaps has the thought, at first fleeting and instantly banished, but gradually becoming more and more insistent, that even prostitutes are more generous in giving than his lawful wife. He is offended by her coldness, at the very moment, perhaps, when she is suffering because he does not know how to rouse her. All this misery results from our policy of silence and decency.

In all these ways, from childhood through adolescence and youth, and on into marriage, the older morality has been allowed to poison love, filling it with gloom, fear, mutual misunderstanding, remorse, and nervous strain, separating into two regions the bodily impulse of sex and the spiritual impulse of ideal love, making the one beastly and the other sterile. It is not so that life should be lived. The animal and the spiritual natures should not be at war. There is nothing in either that is incompatible with the other and neither can reach its full fruition except in union with the other. The love of man and woman at its best is free and fearless, compounded of body and mind in equal proportions; not dreading the physical basis lest it should interfere with the idealisation. Love should be a tree whose roots are deep in the earth, but whose branches extend into heaven. But love cannot grow and flourish while it is hedged about with taboos and superstitious terrors, with words of reprobation and silences of horror. The love of man and woman and the love of parents and children are the two central facts in our emotional life. While degrading the one, conventional morality has pretended to exalt the other, but in fact the love of parents for children has suffered through the degradation of the love of parents for each other. Children who are the fruit of joy and mutual fulfilment can be loved in a way more healthy and robust, more in accordance with the ways of nature, more simple, direct, and animal, and yet more unselfish and fruitful, than is possible to parents starved, hungry, and eager, reaching out to the helpless young for some fragments of the nutriment that has been denied them in marriage, and in so doing, warping infant minds and laying the foundation of the same troubles for the next generation. To fear love is to fear life, and those who fear life are already three parts dead.

Chapter 20

The Place of Sex among Human Values

The writer who deals with a sexual theme is always in danger of being accused, by those who think that such themes should not be mentioned, of an undue obsession with his subject. It is thought that he would not risk the censure of prudish and prurient persons unless his interest in the subject were out of all proportion to its importance. This view, however, is only taken in the case of those who advocate changes in the conventional ethic. Those who stimulate the appeals to harry prostitutes and those who secure legislation nominally against the White Slave Traffic, but really against voluntary and decent extra-marital relations; those who denounce women for short skirts and lipsticks; and those who spy upon sea beaches in the hopes of discovering inadequate bathing costumes, are none of them supposed to be the victims of a sexual obsession. Yet in fact they probably suffer much more in this way than do writers who advocate greater sexual freedom. Fierce morality is generally a reaction against lustful emotions, and the man who gives expression to it is generally filled with indecent thoughts – thoughts which are rendered indecent, not by the mere fact that they have a sexual content, but by the fact that morality has incapacitated the thinker from thinking cleanly and wholesomely on this topic. I am quite in agreement with the Church in thinking that obsession with sexual topics is an evil, but I am not in agreement with the Church as to the best methods of avoiding this evil. It is notorious that St Anthony was more obsessed by sex than the most extreme voluptuary who ever lived; I will not adduce more recent examples for fear of giving offence. Sex is a natural need, like food and drink. We blame the gormandizer and the dipsomaniac, because in the case of each an interest which has a certain legitimate place in life has usurped too large a share of his thoughts and emotions. But we do not blame a man for a normal and healthy enjoyment of a reasonable quantity of food. Ascetics, it is true, have done so, and have considered that a man should cut down his nutriment to the lowest point compatible with survival, but this view is not now common, and may be ignored. The Puritans, in their determination to avoid the pleasures of sex, became somewhat more conscious than people had been before of the pleasures of the table. As a seventeenth-century critic of Puritanism says:—

> Would you enjoy gay nights and pleasant dinners?
> Then must you board with saints and bed with sinners.

It would seem, therefore, that the Puritans did not succeed in subduing the purely corporeal part of our human nature, since what they took away from sex they added to gluttony. Gluttony is regarded by the Catholic Church as one of the seven deadly sins, and those who practise it are placed by Dante in one of the deeper circles of hell; but it is a somewhat vague sin, since it is hard to say where a legitimate interest in food ceases and guilt begins to be incurred. Is it wicked to eat anything that is not nourishing? If so, with every salted almond we risk damnation. Such views, however, are out of date. We all know a glutton when we see one, and although he may be somewhat despised, he is not severely reprobated. In spite of this fact, undue obsession with food is rare among those who have never suffered want. Most people eat their meals and then think about other things until the next meal. Those, on the other hand, who, having adopted an ascetic philosophy, have deprived themselves of all but the minimum of food, become obsessed by visions of banquets and dreams of demons bearing luscious fruits. And marooned Antarctic explorers, reduced to a diet of whale's blubber, spend their days planning the dinner they will have at the Carlton when they get home.

Such facts suggest that, if sex is not to be an obsession, it should be regarded by the moralists as food has come to be regarded, and not as food was regarded by the hermits of the Thebaid. Sex is a natural human need like food and drink. It is true that men can survive without it, whereas they cannot survive without food and drink, but from a psychological standpoint the desire for sex is precisely analogous to the desire for food and drink. It is enormously enhanced by abstinence, and temporarily allayed by satisfaction. While it is urgent, it shuts out the rest of the world from the mental purview. All other interests fade for the moment, and actions may be performed which will subsequently appear insane to the man who has been guilty of them. Moreover, as in the case of food and drink, the desire is enormously stimulated by prohibition. I have known children refuse apples at breakfast and go straight out into the orchard and steal them, although the breakfast apples were ripe and the stolen apples unripe. I do not think it can be denied that the desire for alcohol among well-to-do Americans is much stronger than it was twenty years ago. In like manner, Christian teaching and Christian authority have immensely stimulated interest in sex. The generation which first ceases to believe in the conventional teaching is bound, therefore, to indulge in sexual freedom to a degree far beyond what is to be expected of those whose views on sex are unaffected by superstitious teaching, whether positively or negatively. Nothing but freedom will prevent undue obsession with sex, but even freedom will not have this effect unless it has become habitual and has been associated with a wise education as regards sexual matters. I wish to repeat, however, as emphatically as I can, that I regard an undue preoccupation with this topic as an evil, and that I think this evil widespread at the present day, especially in America, where I find it particularly pronounced among the sterner moralists, who display it markedly by their readiness to believe falsehoods concerning those whom they regard as their opponents. The glutton, the voluptuary, and the ascetic are all self-absorbed persons whose horizon is limited by their own desires, either by way of satisfaction or by way of renunciation. A man who is healthy in mind and body will not have his interests thus concentrated upon himself. He will look out upon the world and find in it objects that seem to him worthy of his attention. Absorption in self is not, as some have supposed, the natural condition of unregenerate man. It is a disease brought on, almost always, by some thwarting of natural impulses. The voluptuary who gloats over thoughts of sexual gratification is in general the result of some kind of deprivation, just as the man who hoards food is usually a man who has lived through a famine or a period of destitution. Healthy, outward-looking men and women are not to be produced by the thwarting of natural impulse, but by the equal and balanced development of all the impulses essential to a happy life.

I am not suggesting that there should be no morality and no self-restraint in regard to sex, any more than in regard to food. In regard to food we have restraints of three kinds, those of law, those of manners, and those of health. We regard it as wrong to steal food, to take more than our share at a common meal, and to eat in ways that are likely to make us ill. Restraints of a similar kind are essential where sex is concerned, but in this case they are much more complex and involve much more self-control. Moreover, since one human being ought not to have property in another, the analogue of stealing is not adultery, but rape, which obviously must be forbidden by law. The questions that arise in regard to health are concerned almost entirely with venereal disease, a subject which we have already touched upon in connection with prostitution. Clearly, the diminution of professional prostitution is the best way, apart from medicine, of dealing with this evil, and diminution of professional prostitution can be best effected by that greater freedom among young people which has been growing up in recent years.

A comprehensive sexual ethic cannot regard sex merely as a natural hunger and a possible source of danger. Both these points of view are important, but it is even more important to remember that sex is connected with some of the greatest goods in human life. The three that seem paramount are lyric love, happiness in marriage, and art. Of lyric love and marriage we have already spoken. Art is thought by some to be independent of sex, but this view has fewer adherents now than it had in former times. It is fairly clear that the impulse to every kind of aesthetic creation is psychologically connected with courtship, not necessarily in any direct or obvious way, but none the less profoundly. In order that the sexual impulse may lead to artistic expression, a number of conditions are necessary. There must be artistic capacity; but artistic capacity, even within a given race, appears as though it were common at one time and uncommon at another, from which it is safe to conclude that environment, as opposed to native talents, has an important part to play in the development of the artistic impulse. There must be a certain kind of freedom, not the sort that consists in rewarding the artist, but the sort that consists in not compelling him or inducing him to form habits which turn him into a Philistine. When Julius II imprisoned Michelangelo, he did not in any way interfere with that kind of freedom which the artist needs. He imprisoned him because he considered him an important man, and he would not tolerate the slightest offence to him from anybody whose rank was less than papal. When, however, an artist is compelled to kotow to rich patrons or town councillors, and to adapt his work to their aesthetic canons, his artistic freedom is lost. And when he is compelled by fear of social and economic persecution to go on living in a marriage which has become intolerable, he is deprived of the energy which artistic creation requires. Societies that have been conventionally virtuous have not produced great art. Those which have, have been composed of men such as Idaho would sterilise. America at present imports most of its artistic talent from Europe, where, as yet, freedom lingers; but already the Americanisation of Europe is making it necessary to turn to the negroes. The last home of art, it seems, is to be somewhere on the Upper Congo, if not in the uplands of Tibet. But its final extinction cannot be long delayed, since the rewards which America is prepared to lavish upon foreign artists are such as must inevitably bring about their artistic death. Art in the past has had a popular basis, and this has depended upon joy of life. Joy of life, in its turn, depends upon a certain spontaneity in regard to sex. Where sex is repressed, only work remains, and a gospel of work for work's sake never produced any work worth doing. Let me not be told that someone has collected statistics of the number of sexual acts *per diem* (or shall we say *per noctem*?) performed in the United States, and that it is at least as great per head as in any other country. I do not know whether this is the case or not, and I am not in any way concerned to deny it. One of the most dangerous fallacies of the conventional moralists is the reduction of sex to the sexual act, in order to be the better able to belabour it. No civilised man, and no savage that I have ever heard of, is satisfied in his instinct by the bare sexual act. If the impulse which leads to the act is to be satisfied, there must be courtship, there must be love, there must be companionship. Without these, while the physical hunger may be appeased for the moment, the mental hunger remains unabated, and no profound satisfaction can be obtained. The sexual freedom that the artist needs is freedom to love, not the gross freedom to relive the bodily need with some unknown woman; and freedom to love is what, above all, the conventional moralists will not concede. If art is to revive after the world has been Americanised, it will be necessary that America should change, that its moralists should become less moral and its immoralists less immoral, that both, in a word, should recognise the higher values involved in sex, and the possibility that joy may be of more value than a bank-account. Nothing in America is so painful to the traveller as the lack of joy. Pleasure is frantic and bacchanalian, a matter of momentary oblivion, not of delighted self-expression. Men whose grandfathers danced to the music of the pipe in Balkan or Polish villages sit throughout the day glued to their desks, amid typewriters and telephones, serious, important, and worthless. Escaping in the evening to drink and a new kind of noise, they imagine that they are finding happiness, whereas they are finding only a frenzied and incomplete oblivion of the hopeless routine of money that breeds money, using for the purpose the bodies of human beings whose souls have been sold into slavery.

It is not my intention to suggest, what I by no means believe, that all that is best in human life is connected with sex. I do not myself regard science, either practical or theoretical, as connected with it, nor yet certain kinds of important social and political activities. The impulses that lead to the complex desires of adult life can be arranged under a few simple heads. Power, sex, and parenthood appear to me to be the source of most of the things that human beings do, apart from what is necessary for self-preservation. Of these three, power begins first and ends last. The child, since he has very little power, is dominated by the desire to have more. Indeed, a large proportion of his activities spring from this desire. His other dominant desire is vanity – the wish to be praised and the fear of being blamed or left out. It is vanity that makes him a social being and gives him the virtues necessary for life in a community. Vanity is a motive closely intertwined with sex, though in theory separable from it. But power has, so far as I can see, very little connection with sex, and it is love of power, at least as much as vanity, that makes a child work at his lessons and develop his muscles. Curiosity and the pursuit of knowledge should, I think, be regarded as a branch of the love of power. If knowledge is power, then the love of knowledge is the love of power. Science, therefore, except for certain branches of biology and physiology, must be regarded as lying outside the province of the sexual emotions. As the Emperor Frederick II is no longer alive, this opinion must remain more or less hypothetical. If he were still alive, he would no doubt decide it by castrating an eminent mathematician and an eminent composer and observing the effects upon their respective labours. I should expect the former to be nil and the latter to be considerable. Seeing that the pursuit of knowledge is one of the most valuable elements in human nature, a very important sphere of activity is, if we are right, exempted from the domination of sex.

Power is also the motive to most political activity, understanding this word in its widest sense. I do not mean to suggest that a great statesman is indifferent to the public welfare; on the contrary, I believe him to be a man in whom parental feeling has become widely diffused. But unless he has also a considerable love of power he will fail to sustain the labours necessary for success in a political enterprise. I have known many high-minded men in public affairs, but unless they had an appreciable dose of personal ambition they seldom had the energy to accomplish the good at which they aimed. On a certain crucial occasion, Abraham Lincoln made a speech to two recalcitrant senators, beginning and ending with the words: 'I am the President of the United States, clothed with great power.' It can hardly be questioned that he found some pleasure in asserting this fact. Throughout all politics, both for good and for evil, the two chief forces are the economic motive and the love of power; an attempt to interpret politics on Freudian lines is, to my mind, a mistake.

If we are right in what we have been saying, most of the greatest men, other than artists, have been actuated in their important activities by motives unconnected with sex. If such activities are to persist, and are, in their humbler forms, to become common, it is necessary that sex should not overshadow the remainder of a man's emotional and passionate nature. The desire to understand the world and the desire to reform it are the two great engines of progress without which human society would stand still or retrogress. It may be that too complete a happiness would cause the impulses to knowledge and reform to fade. When Cobden wished to enlist John Bright in the free trade campaign, he based a personal appeal upon the sorrow that Bright was experiencing owing to his wife's recent death. It may be that without this sorrow Bright would have had less sympathy with the sorrows of others. And many a man has been driven to abstract pursuits by despair of the actual world. To a man of sufficient energy, pain may be a valuable stimulus, and I do not deny that if we were all perfectly happy we should not exert ourselves to become happier. But I cannot admit that it is any part of the duty of human beings to provide others with pain on the off-chance that it may prove fruitful. In ninety-nine cases out of a hundred pain proves merely crushing. In the hundredth case it is better to trust to the natural shocks that flesh is heir to. So long as there is death there will be sorrow, and so long as there is sorrow it can be no part of the duty of human beings to increase its amount, in spite of the fact that a few rare spirits know how to transmute it.

[handwritten marginalia:] I am one. I hope to be successful at it. I do hope my songs will be heard.

Chapter 21

Conclusion

In the course of our discussion we have been led to certain conclusions, some historical, some ethical. Historically, we found that sexual morality, as it exists in civilised societies, has been derived from two different sources: on the one hand desire for certainty as to fatherhood, on the other an ascetic belief that sex is wicked, except in so far as it is necessary for propagation. Morality in pre-Christian times, and in the Far East down to the present day, had only the former source, except in India and Persia, which are the centres from which asceticism appears to have spread. The desire to make sure of paternity does not, of course, exist in those backward races which are ignorant of the fact that the male has any part in generation. Among them, although masculine jealousy places certain limitations upon female licence, women are on the whole much freer than in early patriarchal societies. It is clear that in the transition there must have been considerable friction, and the restraints upon women's freedom were doubtless considered necessary by men who took an interest in being the fathers of their own children. At this stage, sexual morality existed only for women. A man might not commit adultery with a married woman, but otherwise he was free.

With Christianity, the new motive of avoidance of sin enters in, and the moral standard becomes in theory the same for men as for women, though in practice the difficulty of enforcing it upon men has always led to a greater toleration of their failings than of those of women. Early sexual morality had a plain biological purpose, namely to ensure that the young should have the protection of two parents during their early years and not only of one. This purpose was lost sight of in Christian theory, though not in Christian practice.

In quite modern times there have been signs that both the Christian and the pre-Christian parts of sexual morality are undergoing modification. The Christian part has not the hold that it formerly had, because of the decay of religious orthodoxy and the diminishing intensity of belief even among those who still believe. Men and women born during the present century, although their unconscious is apt to retain the old attitudes, do not, for the most part, consciously believe that fornication as such is sin. As for the pre-Christian elements in sexual ethics, these have been modified by one factor, and are in process of being modified by yet another. The first of these factors is contraceptives, which are making it increasingly possible to prevent sexual intercourse from leading to pregnancy, and are therefore enabling women, if unmarried, to avoid children altogether, and if married, to have children only by their husbands, without in either case finding it necessary to be chaste. This process is not yet complete, because contraceptives are not yet wholly reliable, but one may, I think, assume that before very long they will become so. In that case, assurance of paternity will become possible without the insistence that women shall have no sexual intercourse outside marriage. It may be said that women could deceive their husbands on the point, but after all it has been possible from the earliest times for women to deceive their husbands, and the motive for deception is much less strong when the question is merely who shall be the father than when it is whether there shall be intercourse with a person who may be passionately loved. One may therefore assume that deceit as to paternity, though it may occasionally occur, will be less frequent than deceit as to adultery has been in the past. It is also by no means impossible that the jealousy of husbands should, by a new convention, adapt itself to the new situation, and arise only when wives propose to choose some other man as the father of their children. In the East, men have always tolerated liberties on the part of eunuchs which most European husbands would resent. They have tolerated them because they introduce no doubt as to paternity. The same kind of toleration might easily be extended to liberties accompanied by the use of contraceptives.

The bi-parental family may, therefore, survive in the future without making such great demands upon the continence of women as it had to make in the past. A second factor, however, in the change which is coming over sexual morals, is liable to have more far-reaching effects. This is the increasing participation of the State in the maintenance and education of children. This factor, so far, affects mainly the wage-earning classes, but they, after all, are a majority of the population, and it is quite likely that the substitution of the State for the father, which is gradually taking place where they are concerned, will ultimately extend to the whole population. The part of the father, in animal families as with the human family, has been to provide protection and maintenance, but in civilised communities protection is provided by the police, and maintenance may come to be provided wholly by the State, so far, at any rate, as the poorer sections of the population are concerned. If that were so, the father would cease to serve any obvious purpose. With regard to the mother, there are two possibilities. She may continue her ordinary work and have her children cared for in institutions, or she may, if the law so decides, be paid by the State to care for her children while they are young. If the latter course is adopted, it may be used for a while to bolster up traditional morality, since a woman who is not virtuous may be deprived of payment. But if she is deprived of payment she will be unable to support her children unless she goes to work, and it will therefore be necessary to put her children in some institution. It would seem probable, therefore, that the operation of economic forces may lead to the elimination of the father, and even to a

196 Marriage and Morals

great extent of the mother, in the care of children whose
parents are not rich. If so, all the traditional reasons for traditional morality will have disappeared, and new reasons will
have to be found for a new morality.

The break-up of the family, if it comes about, will not be,
to my mind, a matter for rejoicing. The affection of parents is
important to children, and institutions, if they exist on a large
scale, are sure to become very official and rather harsh. There
will be a terrible degree of uniformity when the differentiating
influence of different home environments is removed. And
unless an international Government is previously established,
the children of different countries will be taught a virulent
form of patriotism which will make it nearly certain that they
will exterminate each other when grown up. The necessity for
an international Government arises also in regard to population, since in its absence nationalists have a motive for en-
couraging a greater increase of numbers than is desirable,
and with the progress of medicine and hygiene, the only
remaining method of disposing of excessive numbers will be
war.

While the sociological questions are often difficult and
complicated, the personal questions are, to my mind, quite
simple. The doctrine that there is something sinful about sex
is one which has done untold harm to individual character – a
harm beginning in early childhood and continuing throughout
life. By keeping sex love in a prison, conventional morality has
done much to imprison all other forms of friendly feeling, and
to make men less generous, less kindly, more self-assertive
and more cruel. Whatever sexual ethic may come to be ultimately accepted must be free from superstition and must
have recognizable and demonstrable grounds in its favour.
Sex cannot dispense with an ethic, any more than business or
sport or scientific research or any other branch of human
activity. But it can dispense with an ethic based solely upon
ancient prohibitions propounded by uneducated people in a

society totally unlike our own. In sex, as in economics and in politics, our ethic is still dominated by fears which modern discoveries have made irrational, and the benefit to be derived from those discoveries is largely lost through failure of psychological adaptation to them.

It is true that the transition from the old system to the new has its own difficulties, as all transitions have. Those who advocate any ethical innovation are invariably accused, like Socrates, of being corrupters of youth; nor is this accusation always wholly unfounded, even when in fact the new ethic which they preach would, if accepted in its entirety, lead to a better life than the old ethic which they seek to amend. Everyone who knows the Mohammedan East asserts that those who have ceased to think it necessary to pray five times a day have also ceased to respect other moral rules which we consider more important. The man who proposes any change in sexual morality is especially liable to be misinterpreted in this way, and I am conscious myself of having said things which some readers may have misinterpreted.

The general principle upon which the newer morality differs from the traditional morality of Puritanism is this: we believe that instinct should be trained rather than thwarted. Put in these general terms, the view is one which would win very wide acceptance among modern men and women, but it is one which is only fully valid when accepted with its full implications and applied from the earliest years. If in childhood instinct is thwarted rather than trained, the result may be that it has to be to some extent thwarted throughout later life, because it will have taken on highly undesirable forms as a result of thwarting in early years. The morality which I should advocate does not consist simply of saying to grown-up people or to adolescents: 'Follow your impulses and do as you like.' There has to be consistency in life; there has to be continuous effort directed to ends that are not immediately beneficial and not at every moment attractive; there has to be consideration for others; and there should be certain standards of rectitude. I should not, however, regard self-control as an end in itself, and I should wish our institutions and our moral conventions to be such as to make the need for self-control a minimum rather than a maximum. The use of self-control is like the use of brakes on a train. It is useful when you find yourself going in the wrong direction, but merely harmful when the direction is right. No one would maintain that a train ought always to be run with the brakes on, yet the habit of difficult self-control has a very similar injurious effect upon the energies available for useful activity. Self-control causes these energies to be largely wasted on internal friction instead of external activity; and on this account it is always regrettable, though sometimes neccessary.

The degree to which self-control is necessary in life depends upon the early treatment of instinct. Instincts, as they exist in children, may lead to useful activities or harmful ones, just as the steam in a locomotive may take it towards its destination, or into a siding where it is smashed by an accident. The function of education is to guide instinct into the directions in which it will develop useful rather than harmful activities. If this task has been adequately performed in early years, a man or woman will, as a rule, be able to live a useful life without the need of severe self-control except, perhaps, at a few rare crises. If, on the other hand, early education has consisted in a mere thwarting of instinct, the acts to which instinct prompts in later life will be partly harmful, and will therefore have to be continually restrained by self-control.

These general considerations apply with peculiar force to sexual impulses, both because of their great strength and because of the fact that traditional morality has made them its peculiar concern. Most traditional moralists appear to think that, if our sexual impulses were not severely checked, they would become trivial, anarchic, and gross. I believe this view to be derived from observation of those who have acquired the usual inhibitions from their early years and have subsequently attempted to ignore them. But in such men the early prohibitions are still operative even when they do not succeed in prohibiting. What is called conscience, that is to say, the unreasoning and more or less unconscious acceptance of precepts learnt in early youth, causes men still to feel that whatever the conventions prohibit is wrong, and this feeling may persist in spite of intellectual convictions to the contrary. It thus produces a personality divided against itself, one in which instinct and reason no longer go hand in hand, but instinct has become trivial and reason has become anaemic. One finds in the modern world various different degrees of revolt against conventional teaching. The commonest of all is the revolt of the man who intellectually acknowledges the ethical truth of the morality he was taught in youth, but confesses with a more or less unreal regret that he is not sufficiently heroic to live up to it. For such a man there is little to be said. It would be better that he should alter either his practice or his beliefs in such a way as to bring harmony between them. Next comes the man whose conscious reason has rejected much that he learnt in the nursery, but whose unconscious still accepts it in its entirety. Such a man will suddenly change his line of conduct under the stress of any strong emotion, especially fear. A serious illness or an earthquake may cause him to repent and to abandon his intellectual convictions as the result of an uprush of infantile beliefs. Even at ordinary times his behaviour will be inhibited, and the inhibitions may take an undesirable form. They will not prevent him from acting in ways that are condemned by traditional morals, but they will prevent him from doing so in a wholehearted way, and will thus eliminate from his actions some of the elements that would have given them value. The substitution of a new moral code for the old one can never be completely satisfactory, unless the new one is accepted with the whole personality, not only with that top layer which constitutes our conscious thought. To most people this is very difficult if throughout their early years they have been exposed to the old morality. It is therefore impossible to judge a new morality fairly until it has been applied in early education.

Sex morality has to be derived from certain general principles, as to which there is perhaps a fairly wide measure of agreement, in spite of the wide disagreement as to the consequences to be drawn from them. The first thing to be secured is that there should be as much as possible of that deep, serious love between man and woman which embraces the whole personality of both and leads to a fusion by which each is enriched and enhanced. The second thing of importance is that there should be adequate care of children, physical and psychological. Neither of these principles in itself can be considered in any way shocking, yet it is as a consequence of these two principles that I should advocate certain modifications of the conventional code. Most men and women, as things stand, are incapable of being as wholehearted and as generous in the love that they bring to marriage as they would be if their early years had been less hedged about with taboos. They either lack the necessary experience, or they have gained it in furtive and undesirable ways. Moreover, since jealousy has the sanction of moralists, they feel justified in keeping each other in a mutual prison. It is of course a very good thing when a husband and wife love each other so completely that neither is ever tempted to unfaithfulness; it is not, however, a good thing that unfaithfulness, if it does occur, should be treated as something terrible, nor is it desirable to go so far as to make all friendship with persons of the other sex impossible. A good life cannot be founded upon fear, prohibition, and mutual interference with freedom. Where faithfulness is achieved without these, it is good, but where all this is necessary it may well be that too high a price has been paid, and that a little mutual toleration of occasional lapses would be better. There can be no doubt that mutual jealousy, even where there is physical faithfulness, often causes more unhappiness in a marriage than would be caused if there were more confidence in the ultimate strength of a deep and permanent affection.

The obligations of parents towards children are treated far more lightly than seems to me right by many persons who consider themselves virtuous. Given the present system of the bi-parental family, as soon as there are children it is the duty of both parties to a marriage to do everything that they can to preserve harmonious relations, even if this requires considerable self-control. But the control required is not merely, as conventional moralists pretend, that involved in restraining every impulse to unfaithfulness; it is just as important to control impulses to jealousy, ill-temper, masterfulness, and so on. There can be no doubt that serious quarrels between parents are a very frequent cause of nervous disorders in children; therefore whatever can be done to prevent such quarrels should be done. At the same time, where one or both of the parties has not sufficient self-control to prevent disagreements from coming to the knowledge of the children, it may well be better that the marriage should be dissolved. It is by no means the case that the dissolution of a marriage is invariably the worst thing possible from the point of view of the children; indeed, it is not nearly so bad as the spectacle of raised voices, furious accusations, perhaps even violence, to which many children are exposed in bad homes.

It must not be supposed that the sort of thing which a sane advocate of greater freedom desires is to be achieved at once by leaving adults, or even adolescents, who have been brought up under the old, severe, restrictive maxims to the unaided promptings of the damaged impulses which are all the moralist has left to them. This is a necessary stage, since otherwise they will bring up their children as badly as they were brought up; but it is no more than a stage. Sane freedom must be learnt from the earliest years, since otherwise the only free-

dom possible will be a frivolous, superficial freedom, not freedom of the whole personality. Trivial impulses will lead to
physical excesses, while the spirit remains in fetters. Instinct
rightly trained from the first can produce something much
better than what results from an education inspired by a Cal-
vinistic belief in original sin, but when such an education has
been allowed to do its evil work, it is exceedingly difficult to
undo the effect in later years. One of the most important
benefits which psycho-analysis has conferred upon the world
is its discovery of the bad effects of prohibitions and threats in
early childhood; to undo these effects may require all the time
and technique of a psycho-analytic treatment. This is true not
only of those obvious neurotics who have suffered damage
visible to everyone; it is true also of most apparently normal
people. I believe that nine out of ten who have had a conventional upbringing in their early years have become in some
degree incapable of a decent and sane attitude towards marriage and sex generally. The kind of attitude and behaviour
that I should regard as the best has been rendered impossible
for such people; the best that can be done is to make them
aware of the damage that they have sustained and to persuade
them to abstain from maiming their children in the same way
in which they have been maimed.

The doctrine that I wish to preach is not one of licence; it
involves nearly as much self-control as is involved in the conventional doctrine. But self-control will be applied more to
abstaining from interference with the freedom of others than
to restraining one's own freedom. It may, I think, be hoped
that with the right education from the start this respect for the
personality and freedom of others may become comparatively
easy; but for those of us who have been brought up to believe
that we have a right to place a veto upon the actions of others
in the name of virtue, it is undoubtedly difficult to forgo the
exercise of this agreeable form of persecution. It may even be
impossible. But it is not to be inferred that it would be impos-

sible to those who had been taught from the first a less restrictive morality. The essence of a good marriage is respect for each other's personality combined with that deep intimacy, physical, mental, and spiritual, which makes a serious love between man and woman the most fructifying of all human experiences. Such love, like everything that is great and precious, demands its own morality, and frequently entails a sacrifice of the less to the greater, but such sacrifice must be voluntary, for, where it is not, it will destroy the very basis of the love for the sake of which it is made.

A HISTORY OF WESTERN PHILOSOPHY

Philosophers, Bertrand Russell writes, are both effects and causes: effects of their social circumstances and of the politics and institutions of their time; causes (if they are fortunate) of beliefs which mould the politics and institutions of later ages. In most histories of philosophy, each philosopher appears in a vacuum; his opinions are set forth unrelated except, at most, to those of earlier philosophers. In his *History of Western Philosophy*, Russell tries to exhibit each philosopher as an outcome of his *milieu*, a man in whom were crystallised and concentrated thoughts and feelings which, in a vague and diffused form, were common to the community of which he was a part. By taking a wide view Russell gives unity to his subject and brings out the relations that one philosopher has to another of a different period.

'Bertrand Russell's remarkable book is, so far as I am aware, the first attempt to present a history of Western philosophy in relation to its social and economic background. As such, and also as a brilliantly written exposé of changing philosophical doctrines, it should be widely read.'

Sir Julian Huxley

'It is certain of a very wide audience, and is, in my opinion, just the kind of thing people ought to have to make them understand the past . . . It may be one of the most valuable books of our time . . .'

G. M. Trevelyan

THE AUTOBIOGRAPHY OF BERTRAND RUSSELL

'Three passions, simple but overwhelmingly strong, have governed my life: the longing for love, the search for knowledge, and unbearable pity for the suffering of mankind. These passions, like great winds, have blown me hither and thither . . . over a deep ocean of anguish, reaching to the very verge of despair.'

Thinker, philosopher, mathematician, educational innovator and experimenter, champion of intellectual, social and sexual freedom, campaigner for peace and for civil and human rights, Bertrand Russell led a life of incredible variety and richness. In keeping with his character and beliefs, his life-story is told with vigour, disarming charm and total frankness. His childhood was bitterly lonely but unusually rich in experience. His adult-life was spent grappling both with his own beliefs and the problems of the universe and mankind, and the pursuit of love and permanent happiness which resulted in no less than five marriages. The many storms and episodes of his life are recalled with the vivid freshness and clarity which characterised all Russell's writing and which make this perhaps the most moving literary self-portrait of the twentieth century.

'Among the most glittering literary products of the decade'
Bernard Levin

'These pages are by turns hilarious and deeply moving, sharp and beautiful . . . something better than a book in a million.'
Michael Foot

AN OUTLINE OF PHILOSOPHY

'Bertrand Russell possesses in excelsis a gift not too common among philosophers . . . clearness of exposition. He has never written a book in which that gift was more admirably evident than the present volume.'

Sunday Times

THE CONQUEST OF HAPPINESS

'He writes what he calls common sense, but it is in fact uncommon wisdom.'

The Observer

BERTRAND RUSSELL'S BEST

Selected and Introduced by Robert E. Egner

'the cream of the great man's satire, witty, pungent quotes from a variety of his writings.'

The Evening News

WHY I AM NOT A CHRISTIAN

'He is the most robust as well as the most witty infidel since Voltaire and he cannot fail to sharpen men's sense of what is entailed both in belief and unbelief.'

The Spectator

POWER

'Extraordinarily stimulating . . . it is a subtle, witty and often profound analysis of contemporary human society.'

Leonard Wolf

ABC OF RELATIVITY

'Lucid . . . it affords an ideal introduction to the theories of special and general relativity.'

Nature

Titles by Bertrand Russell in Unwin paperbacks

ABC of Relativity	£3.50	☐
Authority and the Individual	£2.95	☐
Autobiography of Bertrand Russell	£4.50	☐
Bertrand Russell's Best	£2.50	☐
The Conquest of Happiness	£2.50	☐
Education and the Social Order	£2.95	☐
A Free Man's Worship and Other Essays	£2.50	☐
A History of Western Philosophy	£4.95	☐
The Impact of Science on Society	£2.95	☐
In Praise of Idleness	£2.95	☐
An Inquiry into Meaning and Truth	£2.95	☐
My Philosophical Development	£2.50	☐
On Education	£3.50	☐
Outline of Philosophy	£2.50	☐
Political Ideals	£1.95	☐
Power	£2.95	☐
Principles of Social Reconstruction	£1.95	☐
Roads to Freedom	£2.95	☐
Sceptical Essays	£2.95	☐
Unpopular Essays	£2.95	☐
Why I am not a Christian	£2.95	☐

All these books are available at your local bookshop or newsagent, or can be ordered direct by post. Just tick the titles you want and fill in the form below.

Name ....

Address ....

....

....

Write to Unwin Cash Sales, PO Box 11, Falmouth, Cornwall TR10 9EN.
Please enclose remittance to the value of the cover price plus:
UK: 55p for the first book plus 22p for the second book, thereafter 14p for each additional book ordered to a maximum charge of £1.75.
BFPO and EIRE: 55p for the first book plus 22p for the second book and 14p for the next 7 books and thereafter 8p per book.
OVERSEAS: £1.00 for the first book plus 25p per copy for each additional book.
Unwin Paperbacks reserve the right to show new retail prices on covers, which may differ from those previously advertised in the text or elsewhere.
Postage rates are also subject to revision.